The General Theory of Social Relativity

The General Theory of Social Relativity

JOHANNA DRUCKER

THE ELEPHANTS

Illustrations by Johanna Drucker

18 19 20 21 22 5 4 3 2 1

***

Distributed by Small Press Distribution, Inc.

Printed in Canada

***

The Elephants Ltd.
www.theelephants.net

ISBN 978-09953483-6-3 print

Edited by Broc Rossell
Cover design by Drew Swenhaugen
Text design and typesetting by Michael Flatt

A special thanks to Matt Sheridan Smith,
for generative conversations

Contents

Current Conditions

Consider the forces evident in our lives across the personal, social, and cultural realms. Think of the shocking events through which we live and the living shocks that we experience. We can barely account for charismatic success, for the whims of power, the transfer of influence, force of affective connection, popular embrace of ideas, the rise of celebrities, and political occurrences—as well as many other phenomena of the cultural world. Bafflement about such occurrences shows the inadequacy of our understanding, perhaps (at least in part) because explanations that go beyond mechanistic causality are lacking. Established conventions constrict our critical imagination. But these conventions—and the phenomena they struggle to explain—might look very different from a contrarian point of view, one that does not accept the premises of social science epistemologies used in the broader culture, still attached as they are to empirical methods, mechanical explanations, and crude concepts of instrumentalism.

What are these alternatives?

Right now, the impotence of explanation is intensified by the erosion of belief. Political events outstrip our rational imagination. We are witnessing the rise of a perverse nihilism and a grotesquely distorted appropriation of avant-gardism as political action. This is emphatically *not* political art. But these actions demonstrate how easily the tactics of disruption and distraction can be appropriated by the political world. At the same time, within the realm of art practices and activist politics, conceptions of resistance and transformation remain prevailing myths. The desire to believe in actual effect, in agency with direct impact, drives organized actions, marches, protests, letter writing campaigns, and other activities that try to use the machinery of democratic process to effective, even progressive, ends. This is essential; every means of engagement has to be kept alive in the current struggles against the massively powerful force of wanton destruction we are witnessing.

But what good are direct actions in countering mass hallucination? Can marches and protests take apart the seductive appeal of made-up constructs? Can directed activity get any traction on the smoke-screen information of alternative facts, of consensual unreality, on the engineered construction of the never-even-simulacral, but wholly invented? We are grappling with an unexamined expression of the social: the phantasmatic.

These questions and dilemmas suggest an affinity with new materialist and speculative approaches to knowledge and its objects, with their processual and dynamic orientation to ontology and agency.[1] However, their investigations don't go far enough in rethinking cultural systems in terms of quantum and non-mechanistic dimensions. A non-mechanistic physics of social-psychic relations is needed to engage the *social* as a medium, and to understand the ways non-linear cultural systems work through affective (rather than mechanical) processes—on quantum levels as well as visible ones.

In quantum, non-linear systems, all influences follow angles of refraction and work through wave functions at scales and distances that have no relation to mechanistic operations. No communications are direct. They are filtered through the opaque medium of the social field. Social causality is always an oblique force; its operations are governed by complex conditions and conditional complexity to which we will always only have partial access. But we can still create better models of how the social system works. The first step is to define the phantasmatic.

The Phantasmatic

The potency of the phantasmatic exceeds that of spectacle by an exponential factor

The *phantasmatic* is the condition of affective engagement with consensual delusion. It combines the absorptive power of Debordian spectacle with a dimension of the Lacanian imaginary in an explosion of transactional networks, addictive engagements, and hyper-mediation. The phantasmatic also enacts quantum functions in the social field. As individuals, we appear to self-elect to be absorbed into the phantasmatic. But the force of hypnotizing narratives of the meme-stream explanation of events becomes a collective mental theater in which we imagine our relation to those events (which cannot be verified because, by definition, they are constructs, expressions of the very wave functions that bring them into being and us into belief in their existence).

The phantasmatic is neither an illusion nor a simulacrum. The illusion is what we find in the world of Plato's cave, where we take a shadow image for the real until the deceptive mechanisms are revealed. An illusion is a surrogate, a stand-in. In a world of illusion, we can pull aside the curtain of deception. A simulacrum exists without any referent in the real, even as it sustains belief. But the phantasmatic produces artifacts of collective belief that become real, become actualized, as events and conditions, because it is not an image, it is a force. In the phantasmatic, imagined referents become actual, conjured into being by discursive memes whose impact is far more powerful for having no accountability to conscience, ethics, or even self-preservation.

The terrifying consumability of the phantasmatic gives it power and momentum. Because its claim does not have any relation to reason or what is actually lived, it floats as a projection screen in an aether of shared delusion. These are the miasmas of our times, the fulsome manifestations of the social imaginary. And they are working through us, with us, as surely as other forces in the physical world—gravity, magnetism, radioactivity, quantum effects—except that they are the forces of the social universe.

The power of the phantasmatic is affective, not mechanical. Thus the potency of the phantasmatic exceeds that of spectacle by an exponential factor, because the producing machines of illusion/delusion have escalated and its transactional intensity has multiplied in both speed and force. A delusion is an imaginary explanation that we internalize. It cannot be distinguished in kind or quality from the real because (in keeping with the terms of constructivist epistemology) it *is* the real. In a world of delusion, we engage in a voluntary willingness to absorb and submit to belief. These transactions, and the affective fields they generate, use the medium of the social, a psychic aether, through which volatile charges flow. These exchanges are characterized by reciprocity: through and across individuals, media, groups, networks, and systems as emerging and changing ecologies.

Affective alignments have far more power than reasoned ones, and the bonds forged through the systematic production of communication streams works through them—and us—whether we are aware of them or not. We are positioned in those streams as surely as we are positioned in any other system of power relations. The extent to which cultural phenomena are a result, an expression, or a manifestation of these relations—rather than their cause—has to be acknowledged. Trump—to take the most extreme example of our current culture—is a manifestation, an extrusion, as well as an instrument within the polarized environment through which his effectiveness works. We are struggling to find the critical tools for engagement—not to analyze any one phenomena, but to understand the processes of its production.

Formulating the Issues

If the aspiration of the avant-garde was to integrate art into life, it has succeeded only in the most insidious way, by becoming the means through which the world is manipulated as a medium and events are produced to create the real

The language of critical philosophy has many sources, among them aesthetic theory. From Romanticism to the present, the arts have engaged with particular earnestness in the tasks of secular salvation, with putting right the broken world. For artists, writers, and critics, such a task has been almost a given, the starting point, an *a priori* tenet of belief. In this self-appointed role as the conscience of the culture, artists have been dedicated to a utopian vision of their own efficacy. A commitment to subversive transformation through strategic or systematic means has been central to avant-garde and activist work. Tactics and techniques vary, from didactic to resistant, oppositional to autonomous—but the critical practices and languages of aesthetic activity across the modern arts have been marked by a conviction that social change could be fostered by work in the realm of the symbolic. That belief has been institutionalized in mainstream and marginal domains, in communities of practice, academic environments, the publications and forums of critical discourse to such a degree that it goes without question. The prevailing ethos of the arts is a commitment to social progress through work done in the aesthetic realm.

And now? We are confronted with the reality that our faith (the word is deliberate) in the agency of critical thought, like other beliefs to which we have been attached, may be a mere wish, a dream. The very terms on which the idea of art as an agent of change is based—direct opposition, strategic intervention, and critical practice—are constrained by outdated mechanistic models of the symbolic and its operations. Whether or not critical thought has agency, that agency has to be conceived as operating in the realm of the phantasmatic.

To envision this conception, imagine social activity as a billiard ball game, but one being played on a quantum field, governed by constantly fluid factors of directionality, probability, and force. Such a game allows us to visualize only a small fragment of the actuality of play, most of which is governed by forces that do not follow a predictable relation between action and reaction, between what we mistakenly take as entities or objects in physical and social spaces. When the balls are understood as energy bundles with a particular spin and no boundaries, and the table beneath them as a charged field without any solid state holding it in permanent configuration, then our perception of the game changes.

In a similar vein, the theory of social relativity builds on intuitions of the ancients—Buddhists and pre-Socratics—who understood that we not only inhabit a dynamic universe in constant flux but also one in which entities are mere appearances, temporary configurations of forces (as per the tenets of quantum physics and philosophical insight). Mapping these concepts onto the realm of the social, in combination with the fundamentals of indeterminacy of non-linear systems, establishes the framework within which the theory can be modeled. This model is a formulation of the social as a medium and field, a sphere whose activities are governed by affective forces operating in ways that cannot be described in rational (Cartesian) or mechanistic (Newtonian) terms. New critical thinking about the human condition has to borrow from other theoretical sciences that go beyond classical physics.

Why?

Because perverse quantum machinations are now in play, with nihilistic, non-linear, avant-gardist mad scientists of policy launching memes with info-maniacal intensity, meeting the media-verse halfway, finding its vulnerabilities and susceptibilities, receptivities and possible flashpoints of explosion.[2] If the aspiration of the avant-garde was to integrate art into life, it has succeeded only in the most insidious way, by becoming the means through which the world is manipulated as a medium and events are produced to create the real. To repeat: this is not simulacra. Quite the contrary. The result is the production of an event as an aesthetic intervention that becomes real. The conflation of symbolic space and lived experience, and the final extension of manipulative imagination into the domain of perception, is the condition in which we now find ourselves: the *phantasmatic*. A realm of created illusion that intervenes in the real and actual and therefore becomes a part of its fabric—which is ours—not just as beliefs, but as events imagined into being that have actual effects.

A naïvete persists in the notion that the relation between intention and effect in politics and culture is governed by instrumentality, by tools, implements, and machinations. The industries of entertainment, economics, business, and other influence peddling try to engineer outcomes from opinion-making apparatuses. They wish they could. But the processes of adherence, alignment, and interpellation, by which individuals and groups come to ideas, public figures, or narratives of events are mysterious actions. Linear logic breaks down, as surely in the attempt at influence peddling as it does in every other area of human behavior. An inexplicable factor, indeterminate but certainly at work, can be detected in the unpredictability of outcomes. How does it happen, how does one find oneself invested in affective alignments? What is charisma? Why are evident lies effective? What attracts loyal followers to improbable figures? Or are the figures manufactured as an effect of that attraction?

Going back for a moment to the arts—that crucible of imaginative, critical thought—we find a concept of social mechanics usually prevails. Political art imagines itself as potent against real agents, even when they are conceived within the symbolic. But direct and/or directed action misses the mark in taking aim at a phantasm. We need to understand the way phantasmatic phenomena wield imaginary influence and impact.

In the current unstable American environment, power shows an ability to benefit from inconsistency, and to optimize a return on randomness. Political moves show no logic, method, or system. The first step in future political struggle is coming to terms with these changed workings of power, and thus the changed conditions for producing understanding.

No state, no nation, no social contract operates directly on its own terms. Influence moves through the social with the swiftly devastating force of psychic wildfire; epidemics of belief spread fast and far, destroying the social fabric; political operatives, playing the role of leaders, consultants, front office and back-stage figures, are making moves based on lessons taken from the avant-garde—disruption, confrontation, shock effects, outrageous provocation, subversion of the symbolic and its capacity to produce stable meaning. The chief elected official is a meme-producer staging event spectacles for consumption with the hope that they become the real.

Meanwhile the "real" erupts ever more poignantly and aggressively with its own agency—and thus, has to be kept out of sight, off the screens, hidden by the distraction apparatus of regular old-fashioned spectacle. Mass starvation, famine, war, devastation, deportation, and abuse, hide behind daily amusements provided by a showman putting on a play of incompetence that is an effective screen for deliberate systematic destruction. Systematic destruction certainly impacts domains framed by reason (e.g. in undoing environment, financial, and health regulations), but even more profoundly erodes the frameworks of accountability on which reasonable activity functions (e.g. by de-legitimating journalism, legal safeguards, due process etc.). The show—immediate and superficial—is a distraction from addressing long-term changes in domestic economics within global conditions, the end game of the long historical arc of European colonial exploitation of human and natural resources, the crashing final act of Enlightenment era democracy. Protests from the opposition function according to classical models—the negation is entirely constrained by the intellectual framework to which it responds. But neither is "he" an autonomous agent; he (or any highly visible public figure, for that matter) is a phantasmatic manifestation of a crowd that brings him into being through reciprocity. The projections of fantasy fueled by ignorance and anger are potent forces.

Where is agency to come from under circumstances like these? How are we to disrupt the forward momentum of the destruction that threatens? The formulation of the avant-garde and its activist legacies were sincere in their belief that intervention in the symbolic could lead to the restructuring of power. But that will only be possible if the analysis of what power is, and how it works, is adequate. (Disbelief that Trump the candidate disparaged Wall Street while Trump the president promotes its interests and his, for instance, won't lead to the structural analysis of effective deception that worked and works at a mass level.) Hypnotized by the shell game of rhetorical gambits, we are analyzing effects, not causes (to hearken back to the image of the billiard table). We are using the tools of an outmoded intellectual paradigm of cause and effect, of grounds games and influence campaigns. But the phantasmatic operates on a quantum level, at a distance, via entangling forces that galvanize the affective system of social relations. Tapping anger, envy, unrealistic expectations, and deep frustration creates energy that fuels a field of escalating transactional intensity.

Critical Aesthetics

The specificity and variety of experience is a snapshot cutting through constant flux

In the academic field of those who study critical aesthetics, collective intellectual imprinting is long and deep. Many of us got our theoretical training through the history of art and its extension into media, spectacle, images, and discourses. Aesthetics, that branch of philosophy concerned (since its eighteenth-century origins) with attention to perception, is still with us, with modes of distinction now etched as finely as your grandmother's china. We may refine our taste and change our tune, absorb other lineages and traditions, voices and rhythms, motifs and formal structures, practices and their terms of use. But aesthetics also permeates personal engagement with specialized knowledge, even if that knowledge is about *knowing itself*. So we also observe that aesthetics (as *aesthesis*) may not be only a form of knowledge among others, but the paradigmatic example of how knowledge as knowing occurs (as an act of differentiating or distinguishing).

At its core, aesthetics is a process of calling attention—to something, some event, object, sensation, action, some phenomenon. And that act is generative; it produces a critical act of differentiation. This act of attention, here and now, is unique. The specificity and variety of experience is a snapshot cutting through constant flux. But the familiar paradigms of aesthetic activity as a minor field of study or a specialized realm of rarified investigation remain. So do obstacles that impede our ability to grasp the conditions according to which we perceive the very conditions we believe comprise our lived experience. Our concern with intellectual effects like critical differentiation reifies those superficial conditions in our imaginations. Like all flatland creatures, we miss the dimensions we cannot process. We continue to calibrate our aspirations according to the principles of secular salvation, transformation, and recognition that have shaped our thought processes and works for so long—indeed, for lifetimes and for generations. The questions we do not know how ask, the concepts we cannot formulate, perform as constraints.

More insidiously, these limitations assure successes of the forces we do not know how to describe. The aesthetics of politics and the politics of aesthetics weave through this general theory of social relativity. The project asks us to rethink the forces at work in the constructed space we conceive of as "the social." The limits of aesthetics are the same as those of its companion thought-forms: common sense, rationality, individual identity and agency, free will, autonomy, universalized assumptions of value, and the viability or even possibility of democratic process. The roots are deep in eighteenth-century epistemology, grafted onto nineteenth-century political philosophy, and brought forward into twentieth-century critical thought. The attachment to topical and structural connections between aesthetics and politics could be criticized as formulaic, even nostalgic; they operate most successfully in the boutique domains of the academic and art worlds.

But the very tactics developed to "deploy" (I'm using the military term deliberately) activist intervention in the name of liberation are those being used within the very precincts of state power to which they were originally opposed. This is not the same familiar co-optation we have seen in the appropriation of art for commerce and commerce for art, not the simple mixing of outsider stance and insider benefits, but a full-on interpenetration of fields of influence and power in a most corrupt and pernicious manner—as we shall now see.

Non-Linear Politics

Lies have more emotional potency and power than discourse rooted in responsible behavior

In his 2016 BBC documentary, *HyperNormalisation*, Adam Curtis points out that the rise of Vladimir Putin's advisor, Vladislav Surtov, is a perverse triumph of century-old avant-garde tactics of disruption as public spectacle. This phenomenon was not and is not inevitable. Surtov was no more a predictable outcome of the radical innovations of modern art practice than Stalinism was some kind of teleologically determined result of the Russian Revolution. The processes responsible for the emergence of Surtov and the opportunistic receptivity to his manipulations are exceedingly complex.

Same with Trump, whose performances of spectacle without art training are the case that shows the efficacy of these tactics, even without intention, because they are integral to the world of practiced spectacle. This is the state of the art of the state at the end of the era of the democratic nation state. Its fall and dying are not being reflected *by*, they are being made *through* these aesthetic means. The conflation of art practice and political spectacle, so different from the progressive utopianism of a century ago, produces a hardline illusion perpetuating and promulgating violence, upheaval, disruption. Random acts against the established order take a whole new turn that is the opposite of liberation. Headline tactical actions combined with hidden policy statements (rather than strategic interventions) are disruptions designed to consolidate power, not confront it.

That current conditions are so favorable to these machinations could not have been predicted. But their appearance demonstrates two dramatic principles. The first is that strategies have no partisan identity. The radicalisms of both the right and left make use of the same distraction techniques and operate with the same swipe and click interactions. The long-term discourse concerning politics and aesthetics, associated with Marxist thought and its utopian aims, can be appropriated for repression as well as liberation. Resistance is not stamped with a partisan program. The confrontational spectacle doesn't care what you believe in; it can be mediated through the ether of the social and used for any agenda. No difference in values shows as a structural distinction in methods, no matter how extreme they are. The denial of structural racism, negligent genocide, and climate change on the one hand, and endorsement of human rights, social justice, and civil liberties on the other are promoted with the same rhetorical force and using the same systems, networks, screens, and phantasmatic projections.

Lies have more emotional potency and power than discourse rooted in responsible behavior. Psychic-social inflammation is fueled by hyperbolic rhetoric. The complete disregard for any relation to truth is unburdened by any attachments to the real, the actual, the uncomfortable stuff of lived lives and experience. The second principle is that reading symptoms of non-linear social processes as if they can be explained by conformance to systematic laws (natural, cultural, civil, social) is naïve. I have suggested elsewhere that the cultural process of literary activity is stochastic, essentially random, and that the transformations of aesthetics have followed and will follow undetermined lines of emergence that cannot be predicted, only described after the fact.[3]

We need an analytic language for description of effects without direct causes. Perhaps we can borrow from Charles Peirce's category of abduction, which he termed the "discovery" phase of logic, which occurs in advance of being able to formulate hypotheses or laws by which phenomena are "governed" in a system. The blind spot of reason is its consistent belief in consistent explanations. In our unstructured, yet ceaselessly replicated environment, the absence of causal, repeatable, systematic conditions can be dramatically obvious. Abductive methods can describe these conditions, but do not explain them.

This articulation of non-linear aesthetics and politics is not simply a reworking of old art and politics debates, whatever their virtues and shortfalls. Instead, I begin a description of aesthetic activity from a starting point where avant-garde strategies of irrational action have come to be embodied in the emblematic figure of Surtov, the tactics of Trump, and the larger inexplicable conditions of our current culture. Were non-linear forces always operating this way? Did we just not see them because the rational machines kept the social contract in place in the larger order of the first-world civil society?

Depending on one's position, the answer varies considerably. Marginalized, abused, outcast, ignored, disenfranchised sectors of the population see the inequities of a supposedly rational society in clear relief as the darker side of democracy, and its dissolution as the end of the Enlightenment experiment that was blind to inequities built into American democracy. For better or worse, that conception of modern democracy sprung from a commitment to a particular version of Reason, a demographically circumscribed but still radical ambition for a government of, by, and for its people. Currently falling rapidly apart, the system served "its people" in part by (the conveniently repressed) exploitation of resources—human and natural—in a global system of colonialization promoted with the ideological mythos of democracy.

The dark perversity of the Surtov phenomenon's success is compelling. The fame and charisma of his profile speak volumes for the force of affective agency. This concept, like that of non-linear politics, the phantasmatic, the triumphal power of lies, also derived from the description of current phenomena, provides examples on which a vocabulary can be established to enumerate these configurations and perturbations. The non-linearity of the phenomena does not make them unclassifiable, only unpredictable. Think of Surtov as an emblematic figure who, like the monstrous Trump, is an extrusion of the social, showing us how an opportunistic and stochastic expression of potentiality can be made manifest.[4] Climate change denial, creationism, the association of homosexuality with moral error, the fascination with empty celebrity industries—these are other manifestations of perturbances produced stochastically in the social realm. What are the features of these extrusions and how, in seeing the particularities of their manifestation, can we begin to understand the forces from which they emerge, without resorting to the failed mechanical laws of cause and effect?

Receptivity is a constitutive force, not a passive condition. A public figure may be made by channeled attention, fed on it to engorged proportions, even called into being by its force. These figures are not independent agents, free willed and strategic, but are opportunistic manifestations brought to the fore in a social physics of attractors, forces so complex that they couldn't be engineered, or reverse-engineered. These forces are always in play, in or as the medium of the social—but our current conditions of rapid, continuous, reverberating mediation and remediation are creating increased energy that is rarely, if ever seen in terms of scale and effect.

Non-linear aesthetics is not a sufficient term to describe the full potential of social relativity, in all of its complexity, but it does describe the ways current machinations of spectacle, performance, formation and expression take advantage of the production of illusion to use strategies of disruption as distraction. The domains of aesthetic thought encompass the production and consumption of thought forms in representation and presentation, as does social analysis. But a crucial shift allows us to move from critical aesthetics as *political*, to an aesthetic critique of the *social*. What forces of the social sphere move us to performance, and how do they cathect participants through affective means? What dynamics generate the compressive torque of these extrusions? This discussion of non-linear aesthetics is intended to help us identify the relation of artistic practice to the tactics and rhetorics developed in the long last century, now appropriated and deformed to unimaginable activities.

Aesthetic Dimensions of the Social

Our desire for an explanation is nostalgic, and reason, which we were so keen to overthrow, takes on the fallen grace of an antique figure from a culture now remote

Disruptive opposition and non-linearity are not the same thing. The familiar histories of the avant-garde demonstrate that some of its originating impulses were conceived within the frameworks of systematic opposition. Activities of the nineteenth century, socialist movements and projects like the progressive artist guilds founded in the eighteen-nineties through the nineteen-tens, had deliberate goals. They organized systematic alternatives to social ills and cultural inequities arising from industrialization. And the aesthetic movement of the 1890s wove strains of non-oppositional apart-ness into the agenda of artistic identity, when art for art's sake became a rallying cry for autonomy as a strategy of withdrawal. Resistance through insularity allowed (and allows) aesthetic isolation to function as an un-ruled and non-oppositional space where the creation of work has efficacy that is not defined reactively.

By contrast, mechanical opposition imprints from its source as a reaction formation. Imagination was the single transformative agent for human thought—the domain not constrained by reason or logic or convention—but it has been jettisoned in the age of critical aesthetics. Socially motivated or "political" art practices make use of directed actions and opposition strategies in the belief they can have direct effects. Non-linear aesthetics perturb such logical progression; they are not reactive but *generative.*

As the fame phenomena amplified in the nineteenth century, so did the media of production and self-production. This promotion apparatus intensifies meme activities in the field of communicative circulation, and (not surprisingly) the appropriation of the languages and means of mass media is one of the signature hallmarks of the twentieth-century avant-garde. Destabilization and disruption become, in addition to artistic methods, goals in themselves, means and ends. The sheer pleasure of the affront, the "slap in the face of public taste," and a desire to control impact and create visibility, becomes a driving force. *Attention* is the generated outcome and object, publicity is a stunt done in the name of this or that.

In our time event aesthetics have proliferated alongside object-based practices. Conceptual work, with its deep debt to Marcel Duchamp, is built on a critique of institutional practices and conventional assumptions about what constitutes works of art. Duchamp, working to expose the paradigms of his age, called attention to signing, naming, pointing, and displaying as fundamental tactics of art making at the meta-level. But the art world continues to pump out high-end branded product lines, and the academic industry of critical affirmation works in tandem to assure the replication of ideological conceptual apparatuses without much acknowledgement of the complicity that binds them. Much work remains to be done on that issue.

But an aesthetic critique of politics has a different agenda: to expose the affective workings of the performative dimensions of the social as they activate political power. Like stylistic shifts and the emergence of movements, the success of new forms cannot be predicted any more than that of older ones. The non-linearity of aesthetics is evident in the gaps and ruptures, breaks and leaps, of manifesto language and publically staged events. Scatter pamphlets from the sky, as the Italian Futurists did, invite the tradespeople of your bourgeois city to a performance of apparent nonsense, as did Dada artists at the Cabaret Voltaire, or place formally innovative graphics in the factories, as the Russian-Soviet designers did—in every case, the effects cannot be matched to causes. Explanations are like figurative astrological forms mapped onto stellar constellations, connecting disparate dots across time and multiple spaces.

The errancies of Surrealist writing embraced associative techniques. Modern syntax broke conventions (visual, verbal, musical) then built new ones. The tenets of montage and collage promoted fragmentary approaches to the making of a whole through incidental compositional organization. Juxtaposition was a key term in the conceptual toolkit of modern aesthetics and, in its capacious ability to absorb anything into its mode, made the porous boundaries of art and life into a zone of ready transfer and transaction. Like abduction, which reads the effects of such strategies, juxtaposition has no *a priori* ordering terms; what occur *are* effects. Why did we imagine that eighteenth-century rules of order would remain adequate to explain the current social sphere? When the theater of activity is a mediated political arena on the global scale—how are we to manage such unpredictable outcomes? And why did we imagine that only the physical world had quantum dimensions and not the social? Disciplinary boundaries do not advance our knowledge of processes unless the work of one domain is brought to bear upon another. The success of the phantasmatic and the allure of aesthetics have such potency. . . .

If we track forward across the twentieth century and into the twenty-first, taking note of seminal moments, the stepping stones, and landmarks provide a perspective that may also be part a kind of collective screen memory, hiding profound impotence behind an appearance of efficacy. The celebrated moments of the avant-garde, which cannot be explained in a linear manner in any case, are formulations of publicity rhetoric as much as evidence of activist accomplishment. The rise of Futurism and the shock of Dada and Surrealism, for instance, are fueled by a shared momentum that galvanizes attention in the social field—not for their "political" conferences, actions, or accomplishments, but for their discourse of disruption. Social energy attracts social energy, and celebrity success in the arts cannot be predicted any more than events in other realms. Odds are weighted by foundational conditions that make an outcome more or less likely, but still indeterminable. Why should the political realm work differently? The systematic terms developed within the avant-garde (opposition and resistance, invention as subversion, publicity and activism), are applied to the ongoing activity of spectacle aesthetics as politics. Social life continues its non-linear momentum. If success in politics—or aesthetics—could be calculated by some mechanical metric, it could be engineered.

But deviation from mechanistic processes was characterized by Lucretius as "the swerve," the force that kept universal elements from acting as mechanized automata. Multiply that concept exponentially and let it operate across multiple domains, networks, spheres of power and influences—then turn the critical apparatus of aesthetic judgment onto the political sphere. In this present, when the tactics of that long history gain traction in the political world, what blame should we assign to the techniques of the avant-garde? Are we to view its relentlessly inventive modes of imaginative intervention in the norm as a negative?

From where did the capacity for those engineered fantasies emerge? How are culture industries, information pipelines, political processes, and imaginative activities intertwined? How is the sheer daring force of the production of illusion deployed so readily through the massive mediating apparatus of the social and political worlds? And whose receptions create those basins of attraction, whose responding energies promote their hallucinatory power?

The dynamics of social intra-actions are as little understood as those of the quantum worlds of communication and exchange. The avant-garde has paved the way through its enabling of events, and via its contributions to the storehouse of techniques, stagings, darings, its willingness to innovate without regard for consequences beyond effect. No blame can be assigned, no simple line of accountability can be attached to the lineage of aesthetic work, but *somewhere* in these entanglements crossed wires have shorted out and the system of values that was always implicit in the exercise of aesthetic practices has been swapped for destructive motivations. So circuits fire with synaptic frenzy, random patterns appear in the media, but nothing prepares us for what comes next, now, and ahead, because the indeterminate unfolding has no reason for its course of action. It appears, and we cope with symptoms that are not the effect of regular causes. Our desire for an explanation is nostalgic, and reason, which we were so keen to overthrow, takes on the fallen grace of an antique figure from a culture now remote.

Our actual practices need to reflect and acknowledge non-linearity and quantum activity as essential (because the trajectories of intention and the realities of action are mismatched), as do our critical apprehensions. Those of us attached to aesthetics as a zone of intellectual activity that plays a role in political ordering of thought and action must come to terms with the full perversity of our conditions. Forces at work in the world cannot be turned towards positive outcomes through the simple instrumental exercise of will. Even if that exercise remains essential it's insufficient. How do we think and act along lines of unpredictability with the tools of our training and intuition?

These are the present challenges to aesthetics and, or as, politics. Our direction is unclear because directedness is inadequate to the tasks at hand, and effective opposition has to be oblique as well as targeted, if only to include the possibility of outcomes unpredicted in our approach. Though we don't control the weather, our behaviors influence its actions. The same is true in the social atmosphere, our exhalations of thought and intake of ideas. Trying to analyze "what is going on" by doing surveys, counting social media transactions, assessing audience responses and focus groups, is like trying to steer a hurricane by observing windsocks and party streamers.

We have imagined the avant-garde all our lives as a reality, a myth, a heroic struggle, a mode of opposition, a quaint construction, a real possibility, or an exhausted piece of historical machinery. But these conceptions were still governed by concepts of mechanical, instrumental, predictable and controlled agency: actors in networks. We are trying to engage the non-linear character of new tactics of aestheticized politics: distractions that keep attention focused in the wrong place, in a supposed theater of activity that is actually only a smokescreen of projections (not reflections, simulations, but phantasms): affectively forceful manifestations of collective thought.

Much effective action takes place elsewhere—in negotiations of power within the crony club, for instance, in intimate networks and the like. Within the protected precincts of cultural life, where bespoke fashion meets exclusive real estate, neither earnings nor taxes warrant discussion. At a certain scale accountability is so irrelevant it can't be addressed. If the avant-gardist operating the theater is a genius in his sleight of mind, of communicative tricks, their unwitting and complicit participation in the phantasmatic production of events imagined into reality is dangerous. The skills required to take apart the engines of expansion of these perverse appropriations of avant-garde techniques will have to draw on aesthetic principles and critical insights because they, still, have a potency within them, if we release them from formulaic thought. Critics of the actual have slipped into the unfolding spectacle that passes for the real. But to address the phantasmatic we have to come to terms with the complexity of the social as a medium, with the forces of engagement through which its effects and affects occur and work.

The General Theory of Social Relativity

The aggregate effects of affect and attention, distraction or abuse, and so on, create their own field of forces that can be described, in so many words, as the fluid and quantum dynamics of the psycho-social atmosphere

In the past, scholars and critics have created tools of social analysis to describe components of the social world: institutions, systems, mechanisms of communication and exchange, of the production of value and promotion of values, of hegemonic forces and ideological constructions. None of this is *wrong*, but merely inadequate—they're all conceived as discrete components, not dynamic, co-dependent ones. Modeling our understanding of the social on this basis is the same as trying to understand thermal dynamics by examining a heating bill, a furnace, ductwork, and a thermostat (or, as mentioned, a hurricane by a wind sock). The zones of heat and flux in thermal equilibrium can't be apprehended simply by examining components.

Imagine you could actually see, like a mosquito, thermal processes (zones of heat, cold, and their exchanges) in action in the world around you. The complexity of transfer and movement, of equilibrium and entropy, would be dizzying. Large systems and small configurations—from global, interplanetary, and stellar to the micro and nano-scale—would each be operating at different rates of speed and change at every point of observation. Now consider the dimensions of gravity and magnetism, of entanglements at the quantum level, and the picture complicates, again, exponentially.

But (thanks to Heisenberg), we also know your observation would generate its own exchanges. Your attention absorbs energy, while your irritation produces off-gassing or other effluvia. No entity or element within this system will or can appear autonomous. All are engaged co-dependencies in an intricately entangled and infinitely varied dynamic system. Envision the rates of change within these systems, local conditions of resistance or density, areas of frictionless exchange, spikes and troughs produced as incidental artifacts of movement and transference, projection and absorption. Conceive of heat loss as having its own range of possibilities, produced by rapid, deliberate, seductive, magnetic, reluctant, or resistant factors and conditions. Consider the sources of energy in the thermal system, and their interactions at a distance—solar radiation, volcanic eruptions, burning fires and cooling waters, the release of atomic energy and the dissipation through entropic forces, all acted upon by the energies at work in a quantum field without strict adherence to the boundaries of geography or three-dimensional space.

We have no difficulty bringing such a model into being and even in considering the complexities of a physical world that operates according to its elaborately detailed dynamics. Human consciousness in its individual and aggregate dynamics participates in the physical world; it *is* a natural system. The medium of the social is constituted with the same complexity as the elements of other systems. Individuals are not autonomous agents or bound entities; their porousness and degrees of entanglement are many. Social entanglements operate at a distance as well as in proximity, they exist across temporal intervals and spatial gaps, and they work differently under varied pressures and conditions across a range of configurations and relations. The aggregate effects of affect and attention, distraction or abuse, and so on, create their own field of forces that can be described, in so many words, as the fluid and quantum dynamics of the psycho-social atmosphere.

Let's use an example to make this concrete: a man gets up to speak at a conference. We know him. Our knowing anticipates his speaking, and he can feel it. The speaking occurs within the field of anticipation. He embodies the meme-stream opportunities of the moment, almost as if emerging from them. He does not cause the opportunities or their underlying conditions. No one could do that. They are too complicated. But he has a canny ability to catch these social waves. As the event unfolds, the agency of the receptive field meets the dynamic energy of the projective speaker. The intra-action between the two is a dramatic demonstration of participation in a living ecology of social forms and fields. They constitute a situation, and are only distinct enough to act in relation to each other with volatile instability. His talk is a provocation and becomes a major event, a state change and transformation that has repercussions through a much broader field than that the original, spatial configuration of the room. The ripple effects move through the social, that medium of transformative refraction, as well as through electronic communications networks. Just as suddenly Trump is on television, and so is the agency of his receptive field, his audience.

Conjure the image of that "ripple effect" to ask what propagates a wave through the social field. The ripple relies on a medium, a substrate, for its effects to be felt as affective. What does it mean for an event to generate a "buzz"? Social media work across time and space, through multiple dimensions of relativity, via wave propagation. The influence of transactions creates atmospheric perturbances. In the room where the talk takes place, the shifts in posture, body language, exchanged glances, received communications during and after the talk are all creating an atmosphere, a *mood.* Each individual is a medium, a substrate, through which the event takes place and within which it registers even as the whole aggregate of the system constitutes a larger field produced in a social configuration. The coming and going of attention is a calculable physical entity. Exhaustion is one of its measures, a by-product that is evidence of the opacity of the social medium and the expenditure required to penetrate it.

Reflect on the difference between giving such a talk to six people and the same talk to three hundred. The difference in expenditure of energy can't be calculated by simple arithmetic in the same way we determine the cost of three hundred pairs of shoes based on the price of half a dozen. The multiplicity of factors requires far more sophisticated computation to address every aspect of the labor of capturing attention and holding it. A single voice of objection, obstreperous and strident, can polarize an entire room, reorienting its psychic field as surely as an electromagnet asserts its forces on iron filings. We could try to measure these social phenomena: how many points of cultural reference are required to produce identification with the speaker, which rhetorical moves make for optimal impact, how are the time span and frequency of eye contact, direction of voice, orientation of communicative focus all used to pull a field into focus—the list could go on. The physics of communication is an effect of crowd density in which values in every area of interaction, resistance and absorption, shift across the duration of the event; the crowd is a highly mediated large-scale field of networked connections, transacted through electronic, analogue, synchronous, or asynchronous systems. The connections here are social, familial, professional, spatial, incidental, etc. with each network carrying its own valences and potency, areas of amplification and resistance.

To be described adequately, the workings of the social medium must be approached from a theory specific to itself, as a General Theory of Social Relativity (GTSR). In this theoretical formulation all relations are co-dependent, all entities are processes (not autonomous), and forces of affect constitute a field of active agents not controlled by reason or regular laws of predictable behaviors.

This system of the psychical-social can be modeled, as mentioned earlier, as the fluid and quantum dynamics of social atmospheres.

The Fluid and Quantum Dynamics of the (Social) Atmosphere

Social weather is not explicable within the terms of Newtonian analysis

The GTSR depends upon these few concepts—the fluid dynamics of the social atmosphere, and the social as a medium, with quantum dimensions. The concept of fluid dynamics provides a framework for particular actions and forms of social activity to be understood within general rules, and is co-dependent with the general social condition as the constituting medium of cultural life (including politics). The social medium is the replete general condition and the fluid dynamics are the actions and events configured within it. The quantum dimension augments mechanical models.

The GTSR begins with the assumption that entanglements of psychic energy are as real a dynamic as those of any other phenomena, and that mechanical approaches cannot encompass the affective dimensions of non-linear social systems. Statistics do not grasp what affect does and how it moves as a force, nor can they chart rapid changes, upheavals, shifts of mood or whim. Social weather is not explicable within the terms of Newtonian analysis. This assertion (of the need for such a GTSR) would hold true for any scale of human, animal, or species system, from the single to multi-celled organisms of the living earth and beyond. But the current density of physical and social, systems, of the intensification of population and media, of rates of transaction and exchange, all of which permeate the physical atmosphere with waves of communicative force, has created a highly charged and volatile set of conditions that bring the actuality of the living field of social relativity into focus. Never before has the rate of social transaction been so high, or its conditions more volatile. It's impossible now to ignore the conditions that call out for critical engagement.

Communication is a living system of reciprocities, as in the (typical) event sketched out earlier, where energy moves between speaker and group, among participants, and back from the group to the speaker. In the total field the energy cost of communication is always shifting, its equilibrium is precarious—oddly stubborn in some instances, whimsical and fleeting in others. Affectivity and alignment, resistance and distance, change constantly. All communication is mediated, of course, but the use of telecommunications creates distributed and asynchronous fields of alignment and cathexis, and these have their own dynamics. In social dynamics the net sum is never the same as energy put into the system—something is lost, gained, distributed, hoarded, thrown away, gathered, held, ramped up, or dialed down in every image. The theory of preservation of energy does not hold in social systems as it does in those of the physical world. Social thermodynamics, as it were, are fundamentally unpredictable and unstable.

The GTSR sketches principles that are neither laws nor rules. The foundation of the theory lies in conceptualizing the social as a substantive field of forces and dynamics through which energy moves and has effects, a sum greater than the individual parts, which cannot be accounted for merely by assessing the inventory of transactions. The "greater than" has its own dynamics as a system or field or realm of activity that produces effects, holds them, and moves ideas and affect. Teilhard de Chardin used the term "noösphere" to describe something similar, a sphere of human thought analogous to the physical atmosphere. But his formulation did not elaborate the dynamics or agency of social forces, or consider them as fields acting in quantum relations.

The Social Medium as a Quantum Field

These are not magical or mystical forces. The fundamentals of the articulated social system operate as vectors and forces, as waves as well as mechanical entities, nodes whose edges are in continual flux, and whose boundary conditions are always contingent

Hive mind and swarm behavior are tropes of popular culture. What is "in the air," we ask, and the answer comes as themes and topics, waves and whims of thought, opinion, as mood. Cobbled from the news of the day and shifts in temperament, as the registration that at any time things—snatches of thought-form and fragments of communication—drift like threads or strings in the atmosphere as the "air" of social thought. What is that air? Where does it get its bits of information, how transmit them, and how register the changes and shifts in their tone?

Novelists, dramatists, poets, and some sociologists and biologists have explored such principles without necessarily articulating them explicitly. Others have crafted theories of the collective conscious and unconscious, relations of animate and inanimate realms, in every model and variety. Consider the understanding Flann O'Brien had of the merging of a man and his bicycle, the concepts of the *duprass* and the *kerass* configurations defined by Kurt Vonnegut, or biologist Rupert Sheldrake's concept of morphic resonance to explain changes in geographically isolated groups of species. These ideas contribute to a non-unified but essential field of insights into daily processes, and they hint at connections uniting entities (or individuals) as waves rather than as bounded or discrete components, invoking system that is not a sum of parts but an emergent ecology.

These formulations provide terrifying but insightful possibilities in which we are neither free nor willed by our own capacity, but caught in higher order systems to which we have little access, but much allegiance. The hive mind concept, of course, totalizes relations into a singularity, a common oneness, without differentiation or nuance, and swarm behavior makes a physical expression of that collectivity, as if the range of options were either individualism and autonomy or the group think activity of the whole.

The GTSR asserts that an infinite (highly specific, continually varied, but patterned and configured) dynamic of relationships is at work in the constant calibration and shifting conditions of equilibrium and entropy in human relations. These are not magical or mystical forces. The fundamentals of the articulated social system operate as vectors and forces, as waves as well as mechanical entities, nodes whose edges are in continual flux, and whose boundary conditions are always contingent. The principles of the GTSR operate at a variety of scales, from intimate to massive, across a range of proximities and spatial configurations, temporal extensions and durations.

The first principle of the GTSR is the recognition that not only are all media social, but the social itself is a medium. To whit:

◊ The medium of the social is heterogeneous, multidimensional, it has many intersecting, simultaneous, and sometimes contradictory chronologies (temporal activity vectors), and it combines discrete entities and influential forces (each of which is a factor of the other).

◊ The medium of the social is governed by rules of relationality in which the variables are distance, frequency, intensity, and any number of attributes of affect and subtract. The by-products can be outcomes like psychic waste, friction, or effluvia, all of which are affected by and affect the various forces at work and inflect their attributes.

◊ The medium of the social is in constant flux, quasi- and pseudo-equilibrium, and is the embodiment *sine qua non* of stochastic processes and complexity.

In shared understanding, the place where daily news and views are formulated, where decisions about family vacations and what to eat for dinner are made, whether to buy or sell something, take up a cause, hobby, or distraction, to indulge in entertainment or labor, marry, divorce, have a child, take a walk—in those realms insights like these barely register, even for those steeped in skeptical realism, with intuitions of stochastic processes and quantum effects or knowledge of dark social energy and dark cultural matter.

Even those of us who keep track of these constant shifts and plays, these undoings and remakings of the very grounds on which our tenuous grasp of the ephemeral world ravels and unravels, do not imagine our daily existence within the terms of such dynamics. How could we? And yet, these forces and processes are at work in every moment, every sphere, every transaction and interaction of human beings.

The Field of Mediation

We think we could give up our television broadcasts, our twitter feeds, our endless texts and calls, and be "media free", as if media were defined by technological instantiation. But the apparently ineffable, intractable, social realm in which actions, transactions, and occurrences register as significant—from that realm, we can never be free

In our mechanistic perception we imagine media as a technological extension of our senses, as Marshall McLuhan so aptly articulated. We all know that media are social and part of the social world in which they are situated;

techno-deterministic notions have long been banished from our conception of the ways media work. But understanding *the social* as a medium requires conceiving the social—the spheres and systems and processes of all human communicative exchange—as media. In the familiar critical framework media are understood as things—discrete, functional, systems or objects, substrates and processes. Even when their role is construed as constitutive rather than transmission-based (as creating and making communication as effects of their specific activities rather than delivering units of communication), media and mediation are understood as discrete. We imagine we can turn away from them—we think we could give up our television broadcasts, our twitter feeds, our endless texts and calls, and be "media free", as if media were defined by technological instantiation. But the apparently ineffable, intractable, social realm in which actions, transactions, and occurrences register as significant—from that realm, we can never be free. We are always participating elements of a living system.

It's time to recognize the self as a mediating substance, that we are a medium, fundamentally, primarily, first and foremost. Humans are a substrate; we do not merely interact with external systems, technologies, or extensions. To say we don't perceive these media and mediating actions would be to deny love at a distance, reactions that cross time and space, the power of crowds in physical or virtual spaces, or the passions of groupthink in all their peril.

The post-Cartesian position (i.e., the limits of reason as an explanatory framework) is familiar in the humanities, but the post-Newtonian (the limits of classical mechanics to explain indeterminate processes) is not. The approaches of new materialist, speculative realist, and complex systems, with their notions of co-dependencies, intra-action, and emergent contingencies, provide a basis for a constitutive theory of mediation and knowledge. The French term, *éspace,* is useful here because it gives substance to the space of exchanges. For instance, the *éspace* of a marriage is the sustained sum of exchanges: moves towards or away, and so on, made in the relations between two people, and can be described but cannot be lifted out from them as an independent structure. The entanglement of participants and connections is complete.

In the mechanistic worldview, media are objects and technologies just as atomic particles were once conceived as tinker-toy architectures. We imagine that when we use a phone, watch a television, and work on a computer these objects remain discrete from our social identity, mere instruments we use. But the workings of these media occur within the larger whole, the field of the social, where the discreteness of the techno-objects is subsumed by the forces at work in the field. Media have dynamic effects, they draw us out, spread us thin, distribute us through their systems and capacities. Media are dynamic forces that engage us in a network of energy exchanges.

Within this framework, media artifacts are no longer instruments to be operationalized, but rather constituted by the very system within which they appear to function as autonomous things. In the GTSR we shift from a mechanistic or declarative model of media (in which media are equivalent to objects and things) and knowledge representation (categories of description and identification), to the performative or generative concept of production (in which mediating ecologies constitute a social system and we are constituted relationally, co-dependently, within it).

This leads to the realization of the social as a primary medium which is the field, the site of record and trace, the emergent atmosphere of exchange, the web of interrelated glances, or shared interests, and acknowledgements, seen, heard, felt forces and vectors of shifting mood, judgment, and assessment. The elaborate transactional conditions and circumstances in the fluid dynamics of social life may seem intractable, but they have to be conceived as a mediating system that is not defined by or constrained to media in a literal sense, but as the constitutive system of social relations.

Tenets of Social Relativity

Absolute zero in the social world is merely denial

By now, the foundational principles of the GTSR should be clear: The observation of real events and circumstances reveals many dimensions of social occurrences, but never all. Newtonian physics explains the world according to laws that operate with systematic regularity at certain level of observation, but at both the atomic level and cosmic level such laws do not hold, as the discoveries of quantum theory and relativity made clear a hundred years ago, when the study of forces, effects, relationships, and influences moved physics beyond the analysis of mechanistic, repeatable, predictable causal relations. The three laws of inertia, acceleration, and reaction hold in physical space at a particular scale. They explain nothing at the quantum level where the phenomena are not deterministic. We term them non-deterministic because we can only describe effects, not causes or direct outcomes, hence the need for abductive approaches.

Likewise, many phenomena of the social can't be explained in the common understanding of cause and effect, even in specialized languages of social sciences and their corollary terms and fields. We cannot—do not—see processes that occur in other dimensions or are brought about through the non-mechanical forces of social relativity. This does not mean they do not exist. The impacts and effects are often dramatically visible. Our explanations have been inadequate to account for the complexity of the phenomena to which we are constantly subjected and whose effects work through us constantly. Just as surely as ultraviolet waves, magnetism, neutrinos, particles, and phenomena are actively present without our attention to their effects, so are the processes of social relativity at work in the medium of social relations.

Theories of cognition, as well, have extended beyond the mentalist model of an individual's experience as an embodied mind, to include ecological conditions in which awareness takes shape and by which cognition is imprinted. So we don't have to strain ourselves to imagine or conceive of a self not defined by another, not created through alterity, but in a condition of *among-ness.* Constitutive positioning in the social world is governed by complex forces, conditions that come into being and vanish, leaving only memory traces, traumas, or after-thoughts. Absolute zero in the social world is merely denial. Physical entropy is the measure of how much thermal energy per unit is not available for work.

These items provide a set of metaphors for social relations. In any social situation, entropy comes and goes, the work being done at any moment is incalculable if it includes the labor of getting along with others, creating consensus, synchronizing plans and activities, and all the other tasks of dealing with human beings in a social way. Multiple dynamics exist simultaneously in the social systems.

Social relativity is so complicated that it makes atmospheric dynamics look elementary by contrast. Crosscurrents of emotions change more rapidly and dramatically than those of wind sheers and down bursts, cutting through far more complicated and multi-dimensional fields. We do not have one weather, but the complex mix of individual and social dynamics always all in play.

Some features of the social world are analogous to those of the physical world.

Inertia, for instance, is a powerful force in both, perhaps even the strongest force. The inertia of couples, of institutions, of configurations are all very potent in their resistance to change. This seems more Newtonian than relativistic, and yet the causes of social inertia are psychic, not mechanical. (No paranormal implication is meant by the use of the word *psychic.* It refers to the realm of the psyche and its individual and social workings, without the social science overtones associated with "psychology", which is a *logos,* a logical knowledge discourse.) Inertia gains stability by resistance to change, not by fixity, certainty, or immutability.

We can also deploy analogy and metaphor as two generative principles for developing the vocabulary and concepts of the GTSR, but we must keep in mind the physics of social systems is a quantum, and so indeterminate one. The conditions according to which we perceive the conditions we believe to be conditions of our lives are always in flux; a central parallax and paradox of the human condition is right there. The nuanced particulars at different levels of granularity, like those of physical systems, are amplified by the capacity of social forces to act at a distance, without any mechanics of connection (and yet with considerable impact).

Intellectual frameworks that are explanatory constructions (e.g. geology, sociology, politics, economy, history) share a blind spot. They describe contingencies as if they were certainties, and processes as if they were entities. None of this is news. Lucretius knew it, Giambattista Vico knew it, and whole hosts of late nineteenth and early twentieth century artists and philosophers and writers knew it, and railed against the instrumentalization of power in knowledge formations whose constructedness went largely unacknowledged. The imaginative poverty of empiricism has been no obstacle to its absorption for explanations or control of many apparent aspects of the physical and social world.

The GTSR depends on the recognition of the situated, partial, fragmentary, and dynamic mutability of the conditions of knowledge. All and everything operates within certain (in)constant limits and principles.

Making toast in the morning, do we consider whether the concept of heat death applies to the crumbs soaked in butter we lick from the knife? Settling into the soft bed at night, do we wonder how each gentle toss ripples through the atmosphere, how the earth's body shifting its axis ever so slightly so that alignments of gravitational force also alter continuously in ways that over time add up to the difference between one cataclysmic event or another? No, no more than we feel the gradual seepage of identity and boundary loss across the marriage bed and multiple other zones that constitute the space or *éspace* of the blurring mergers. Speaking the name aloud of some absent beloved, do we imagine that thought form expressed has an immediate and spooky influence—from any distance?

These modes of connection do not depend upon the same rules of time and space that govern flossing of the teeth and washing of the floors. Or do they? Perhaps, in some larger framework of understanding, the forces that work equally in all things (or are at least always potentially available to some equal degree). Physical quantum phenomena are not visible at human scale, but the phenomena of social quanta are perceptible everywhere, as soon as we know how to name and describe them.

Basic Formulation of Relations

The basic formulation of relations is highly generalized, and the conditions in which it holds are subject to infinite variation. These conditions can be described in terms of a number of different components, each of which contributes to the dynamics of the system

The most basic formulation of the GTSR is deceptively simple: any and every relationship will "work" (that is, reach a condition of psychic equilibrium) given the right relation between proximity and frequency.[5] In some cases, the distance will have to stretch to infinity and the frequency shrink to zero, but in all circumstances a relationship gets out of balance if the proximity or frequency exceeds the equilibrium conditions. Some of us are more sensitive than others to shifts in the equilibrium conditions. A long car ride with an acquaintance, a vacation with a family member, a retreat with colleagues—these are pressure cooker situations that quickly show how much flexibility there is in a particular relationship's calibration. The addition of other persons and/or changes in the spatial configuration (e.g. a shared room) alters the calculation, sometimes dramatically. Predicting the outcome of adding another person into a system can serve to distribute energy transactionally, to deflect focus and intensity, or to cause a spike of irritation that produces tensions.

As in any complex system, the granularity of description is inexhaustible—the micro-zones of the human condition are subject to friction, drag, whim, and vectors of change at a scale that is almost below the threshold of perception. Similarly, the macro-zones, equally imperceptible, operate at a scale that makes their activities invisible by virtue of scope, scale, and rates of change from extremely slow to extremely fast. Macro processes and micro processes are at work in the social world, just as the understanding of these phenomena shift from mechanical to quantum descriptions in the physical world. This should not seem surprising; what *is* baffling is why it's taken so long to formulate an adequate system of description and explanation.

The basic formulation of relations is highly generalized, and the conditions in which it holds are subject to infinite variation. These conditions can be described in terms of a number of different components, each of which contributes to the dynamics of the system. The enumeration of these as logical categories is finite. But when experienced, rather than elaborated as abstractions the particular situations are infinitely varied. A high degree of specificity and an infinite range of variety are features of all actualities, of course, but logical categories and relations can be generalized by structure and formal features of the relations or situations they describe. Thus, one may be married or not, but no marriage is the same as another, or even the same as itself in any particular moment; nor is an entity with self-evident features or qualities, independent of the experience of the persons involved. But even they have no objective perspective from which to perceive the marriage as an entity. That a marriage exists can be verified, of course, but non-contractual relationships are much more difficult to verify and categorize. The distinction between contractual and non-contractual relationships is logically unambiguous, even if actual relationships may blur these lines of distinction.

Within the general principles stated above, concepts describing the system fall into several basic categories. They are: A) event types (transactions, occurrences, incidents, originating charges, and configurations); B) forces (normalcy, inertia, diffusion, etc.); C) attributes of systems (unboundedness, among-ness, within-ness etc.) D) analytic/descriptive methods (affective metrics, attention to the actual etc.)

A. EVENT TYPES

In effect, the entire unfolding of human social behavior is, in a logical sense, able to be described as "the" defining incident of human existence

Events comprise one of the basic categories in the GTSR. The familiar, vernacular, uses of the term "event" provide examples on which the more general, abstract, concept can be defined. At the highest level of description an event can be understood as a change in the state of something (e.g. water to steam, alone to accompanied, asleep to awake). Any discernible shift in condition from one state to another is an event. Some events are socially sanctioned and culturally codified, such as graduation, divorce, or starting a new job. Others are temporally bounded, such as eating a meal or taking a walk. But any situation in which a state change can be registered is an event. Being on one side or another of eating a piece of toast makes that an event. But for the purposes of social relativity, an event is a situation in which a relationship registers a shift. This could be a positive, minor, shift, such as a simple affirmation of a connection, an assignation, or coordinated plan. It could be negative—a disappointment, betrayal, or serious violation of trust. It could be more or less dynamic, involve equal or unequal participation, and have different degrees of impact on the individuals and the system of relations that connects them. But it is always a shift in conditions of equilibrium.

The list of event types is comprised of five very general categories each of which is, in part, defined by its relation to and distinction from the other: 1) Transactions; 2) Occurrences; 3) Incidents; 4) Originating Charges; and 5) Configurations. Transactions, occurrences, and incidents are the three basic categories of social processes and contain charges, configurations, and effects like normalcy, equilibrium, diffusion, dilution, and intensification.

A.1 Transactions

Every exchange of information, communication, energy, material, chemistry, emotion, force, or any other substance or essence between or among human beings is a transaction. It is an action or exchange across entities, a transfer of energy. Transactions are the greatest force in the social sphere, and can be causal, incidental, or entangled. That is, something may change on account of a transaction (a person is invited to apply for a job) or incidentally (a person may take a new apartment and then appear on a street corner at a particular moment to be hit by a car). A look or glance may compel an action, randomly but with effect, and the action could take place at a distance. The first transaction is causal, the second incidental, the third entangled. All transactions in the system of *social* relativity involve human beings, or living beings (pets and other animals should be included among the transacting agents, given their affective charge). But within a larger ecological framework of relativity, inanimate elements factor as well.

The typology of transactions can be enumerated endlessly. But transactions can be classed on the basis of whether energy is added or removed, whether that energy is negative or positive, and whether the exchange outcome is balanced. In a negative transaction, energy is decreased: one party or group may suffer loss, or, the entire situation may be characterized negatively. In a positive transaction, energy is increased. However, increase and decrease are not inherently positive and negative. An increase in energy could be found in friction, annoyance, or harassment, among other by-products. The removal of difficulty or diminishment of anger is a net loss, but might have a positive spin. Subsets of transactions are actions like *suction, gift, protection, diminishment, affection, admiration* and so on. Transactions can introduce *spin, wobble, a vortex, a downdraft,* and so on. They are subject to the laws of social physics and their specificity is inexhaustible, though the general types can be defined in terms of the polarities (positive/negative), intensities (high/low), and net outcome (gain/loss). Even the simplest exchange—such as a greeting between co-workers—is a transaction with a measurable polarity, intensity, and outcome. Each person enters and leaves the transaction with a slight change in their equilibrium, however miniscule, because they have transacted an event.

Occurrences are a higher order description of the transactions in the social system. Occurrences are made of transactions and transactions create occurrences. But occurrences can be described as dynamically configured event spaces, while transactions are linked to human beings.

A.2 Occurrences

Occurrences differ from transactions because they can be described in their dynamic configuration independent of the individual players involved. Occurrences do not happen without human beings, but their formal properties can be described in terms of dynamic forces and configurations. Like incidents, they are transitory but distinctive. Neither incidents nor occurrences have discrete boundaries, but they do have start conditions and end states, points at which the registration of their existence approaches imperceptibility or insignificance in the scale that apparently matters.

These are all relative parameters. An occurrence might be a flutter of activity in an office. This need not have a single transaction at its core, or even be comprised of exchanges, but might be a ripple in the field of concentration and attention. An occurrence might have a physical cause—a door is opened and air moves through a space, sound is produced, and the human beings in the space all momentarily break from their tasks, turn their attention elsewhere, and then have to reintegrate their attention into their work. An occurrence has taken place.

Occurrences can be enormous in scale. A battle is an occurrence, as is an election, a news event, a party, or a job search. Occurrences can be large events, with many components and parts, hyper-events, but they can also be micro-events—the disturbance of air just described. If an event is a state change and a transaction is an exchange among living entities, then an occurrence is a framework for grouping transactions of a large event space together at any scale. The term occurrence describes the event space while transactions refer to the human exchanges and outcomes.

A.3 Incidents

An incident is a twist of configuring within the continuum of an occurrence. An incident can be a transaction, but it does not have to involve exchanges among living entities. An incident can be as small as a trace, a hint of a possible event. A nod across the room in a crowded space, a dog walker pausing in front of a house, a car stopping suddenly to let another proceed—these are incidents. Incidents register in the experience of an entity, an unbounded individual. Though it might have enormous impact, an incident is a small occurrence. Though slip or a fall might be an incident, its effects on an entire system of relations could be enormous over time.

An incident is always marked by dynamism. As an event it necessarily registers change. But the change made by an incident might also relate to or register against the stability of a configured state. In fact, an incident might be the first fold, disturbance, or perturbation configuring in the immanence of sociality. The point is that it configures; it becomes figured and is thus tractable in its configuration. I can refer to it. "Remember the incident on the patio?" or "Did you see the accident in school last year?" Incidents are highly specific, but the conditions as to what constitutes an incident are extremely general.

Though incidents are not stable, they can be grasped and registered as a figure, that is what is meant above by saying they are a *fold* or other *perturbation* that *configures* – becomes figured. Incidents are a primary feature of sociality. We live from incident to incident, and are ourselves features of and participants in the production of incidents. While an incident can have no autonomy as such, cannot exist independent of its constitutive conditions, its configurations can be described in the abstract, schematically.

A study of the schematics of incidents, an elaborated typology, would have a logical unfolding that begins with the first order of perturbation and builds to incomparably higher orders of complexity. The lowest order of incident can be described as anything that initially registers upon the social. The highest order, while the same in kind (that which registers), can be exponentially more complex in its specifics. No limits on the complexity of unfolding (outward appearance and perceivable configuration) and infolding (psychic effect and interior resonance), perturbing (intervening in a pre-existing state) and configuring (coming to have a specific form), can be established.

In effect, the entire unfolding of human social behavior is, in a logical sense, able to be described as "the" defining incident of human existence. At incident (a configured form of unfolding and infolding in the whole) can be usefully distinguished from an event (a state change in the conditions within which incidents occur). The vernacular understanding of incident, like that of event, transaction, and occurrence, is well developed. We have a good intuition of what constitutes an incident. And an incident, as a configured perturbation of unfolding / infolding resonances, like that of any event, could be modeled and calculated mathematically, though the descriptive effect is more useful than a metric in this, as in many other aspects of social relativity.

A.4 Originating charge

A charge is an initial event, an initiation or start condition with force. This might be as simple as a comment, a remark, a conversational exchange, a glance, a look, a small action, an affront, a compliment, an affirmation or a defamation. Once it occurs the medium of the social amplifies, distributes, diffuses, dilutes, or intensifies its effects. Needless to say, calculating all of the variables and (in)constants in such equations requires acutely non-linear calculations.

A.5 Configurations and configuring

A configuration is not an event. It is an effect or by-product of configuring, which is a state-change. The term configuration refers to the peculiar capacity of entities to identify with each other as a unit or arrangement through time, and to appear to have a logical or semantically significant relation to each other. The spatial organization of a configuration can often be deceptive, analogous to the way constellated figures are comprised of stars whose apparent proximity in the projection of the sky is belied by actual distance across vast areas of space.

But like constellations, configurations assume the appearance of relative stability for some period and can thus be read in their spatial arrangement through the basics of spatial logic—through proximity, hierarchy, similarity, and so on. Configurations can be comprised of entities—a set of transactions, occurrences, or events can constitute a configuration. But human beings can also be configured in relation to each other, bound by position, circumstance, bonds of kinship or contract, or other stabilizing frameworks. A class, a study group, a team—but also people on a bus, in a park, a movie theater, on a crosswalk, at a stop sign, in an elevator, a neighborhood, a café, or even a square mile of ground, are in configurations. A configuration does not have to be deliberate. It can be incidental in its formation but significant in its form.

One of the most curious features of social life across time is the unpredictable duration of configurations. When you come into any situation—a new home, job, or group of friends—the persons with whom you have the most immediate connection and form apparent bonds may not be those with whom a connection endures. The circumstances and entities that seem most present may also vanish and less obvious features of the system become evident. Apparent bond strength and duration of bond are almost never the same. An acquaintance who appears marginal, ephemeral, even distant, might actually stay connected for much longer than one who appears immediately close and engaged (and so lovers vanish, friends remain). The energy in these systems of relations is also varied, and consumed at different rates. These factors should be discussed, however, within the next section, which deals with forces.

B. FORCES

What is the social aether that operates so effectively? Where and how does the thick atmosphere exert its pressures, hold its charges, and its forces? This is the social field, the wave condition of its emergent form and force

Events constitute a category of structural concepts of the GTSR, forces comprise the dynamic concepts defined by the quality of their effects. The basic forces at work in social relativity are 1) Inertia and 2) Affective Dynamics. All other forces work within these. Thus many other forces can be identified as part of the system of social physics—attraction, repulsion, seduction, momentum, resistance, repression... the list could be long. They are subject to a great many modifying and complicating

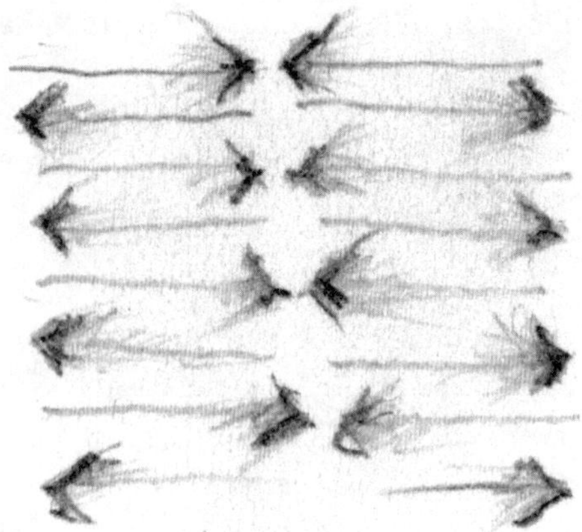

Inertia

factors, work in proximity and at a distance, and work together to produce results. But it is the basic power of inertia (one of the chief effects of which is the force of normativity and its surface appearance, normalcy) and affective dynamics that negotiate the balance between relative stability and volatility.

B.1 Inertia

Inertia keeps couples together long after all fissionable energy has gone out of the system, it preserves institutions against change (for better for worse), and it keeps policies on track, and generally keeps processes in play within configured forms. Inertia works dynamically rather than statically, always as an active force and not a passive abdication of activity. Inertia is the strongest single force in any system, physical or social.

Theories of agency tend to overlook the colossal potency of inertial force. The agency of inertia can appear to be unwilled, undirected. Look again; a sinister dark intentionality, often

preservative, sometimes obstructionist, inheres in such apparent passivity. Nothing *happens.* What does "happens" mean? Inertia, though it sounds mechanistic, is produced by engagement and therefore deeply relativistic. Inertia does a great deal of work in the social systems and holds many configured features of a system from dissolution. Nonetheless all systems and figures are always either decaying or being rebuilt, are in a state of degeneracy, decadence, obsolescence or vague ascendancy. Qualifications on processes are an integral element of the GTSR, and just as all relationships can be calculated in terms of details, so all processes have to be understood in terms of energy, coefficients, and qualifications.

B.2 Normalcy

Normalcy is both a symptom and effect of inertial social equilibrium, and one of the strongest forces within the domain of social relativity. Normalcy is the appearance of "what is", a skein pulled over actual complex and changing conditions in which particulars vary from their means, medians, and averages.

Normalcy is produced when the assumptions (or operative values) of any number of individuals in a group relative to population density (geography, proximity, rates of contact and exchange), modified by deviation from the norm, is calculated as a demographic variable (a similarity / dissimilarity index).[6] Normalcy emerges in the duration *of* a set of conditions calculated against internal changes *to* the conditions. Normalcy is perturbed if radical shifts in demographics occur, but will remain remarkably stable (and repressive) if the system's composition remains the same. Repressive forces generated by normalcy are perceptible, and are in fact an obvious problem. Normalcy is the acceptance of slavery in one generation, animal abuse in another, subjugation of women or prohibition of homosexual acts as part of a status quo.

B.3 Normativity

Normativity is produced as a process of socio-dynamic equilibrium. The thermodynamics of human systems follows some of the same laws as those of physical systems, but with this difference: the communicative medium is not apparent, because it is *us.* We are the medium through which the effects of normativity are achieved and distributed, and we do not need physical proximity for forces to flow, even though proximity relations perform their own very specific and powerful actions. Normalcy and normativity are distinguished. Normalcy is the deceptive presentation of repressive averaging and normativity is the process by which normalcy comes about.

Normativity is a function, an ongoing process and effect of social conditions. It has agential force, and operates as

Normativity

controlling and calibrating instrument of behavior without any obvious or evident existence. It is as strong a force as gravity (as are other social forces, when they are in play), but like gravity it is so integrated into daily life and function that it simply appears to be part of what is in the world we inhabit. The assumptions of normativity are pervasive and even invasive in their regulation of individual behaviors and the registration of violations. If we understand normativity as an exemplary case of the GTSR then features of that analysis can be extended to many other dimensions. The specificity and variety of formations within the field of social relativity are as infinite and inexhaustible as the flux within particulars characterizing daily life among different groups in different spaces, situations, conditions, and circumstances. Therefore, simply stated as modeled above, normativity is an equilibrium formation.

I first encountered the force of normativity in the psychic atmosphere of Charlottesville, Virginia, a small university town where I lived for almost a decade. Because of its size, its relative homogeneity, its controlled realms and networks, it was an ideal site in which to observe and experience normativity. I felt the repressive and coercive force even when I was not engaged in conversation or social activity, on the streets, in the roads, in the tones my voice was expected to emulate.[7]

The force of that coercively structured receptivity was repressive and inescapable. It pervaded meetings and exchanges, every human and physical intersection was blanketed by its smothering effects. What was and was not acceptable, was assumed, and was used as a measure of judgment. The terms were clear: family life was sacred and tantamount, the highest value was placed on its sanctity; homosexuality, though tolerated, was deemed best when it conformed to the terms of domestic partnerships that aligned with family values; eroticism outside of marriage, and any form of non-family intimacy was dangerous and to be contained; and in particular the free-ion agency of unmarried women was deemed a threat.

Because men at any age could be brought into the family bonds, used to impregnate, reproduce, and be entered into the bonds of marriage, they did not have to be contained within the same constraints as unmarried (and in particular older but still sexually viable) women. Young women who were unmarried but submissive to those expectations, living on an assumed trajectory of marriage and family bonds, were tolerated as long as they did not deviate too far from the norms. Because networks of alternative culture were so restricted, lifestyle choices were as well. Straying from the path, deviation from the norm, was met with internal exile, exclusion, isolation, a punishment of unacceptability and rejection. The liberal equilibrium could not tolerate anomalous thought.

What is the social aether that operates so effectively? Where and how does the thick atmosphere exert its pressures, hold its charges, and its forces? This is the social field, the wave condition of its emergent form and force.

The physics of the social system, barely acknowledged and hardly understood, is nonetheless strongly felt. If comparable physical phenomenon were being examined, one in which entities with complex energy types were all in motion and interaction with each other within a confined or semi-confined space, the potential for description would be evident. For instance, imagine five spinning tops and a gyroscope, each made of a different material and density, turning at slightly different rates, heated to different temperatures, and engaging the air with a range of resistances and frictions, and so on. Detail the physical properties to a high degree of specificity (variation and difference in properties) and complexity (rates of change and emergent conditions) and now calculate the fluctuations in the system of the whole. Imagine this system within a contained space, like a box, or one that is open on the top, like a yard, or in an unbounded space, like a field. In each instance the features of the environment would factor into the way the system's energy was distributed. No one would question the reality of or even empirical evidence contained in such a system. The forces at work in human beings are far more complicated, as the emotional factors complicate and contribute to the physical, and the interactions are volatile, subtle, constantly in flux, and too complex to calculate with any reliability. But that does not mean they are not present.

Normativity is a force, not just an effect, a living set of conditions in flux and in codependent emergence with the conditions and entities that bring it into being. Like any other force in the system of social relativity, normativity can be calculated. Like all forces its components are only temporarily stable. Normativity is an equilibrium condition of a complex system, and thus its force is due in part to temporary stability across a certain duration and extension. The components of normativity begin with population size, density, degree of connection (frequency, intensity, spatial proximity, demographic proximity), distribution in space and degree of containment (homogeneous population in a valley or geographically delimited space to heterogeneous in a large, multi-dimensional, and multi-access point environment). Leads in and out of the normativity field make a difference, as do routes of traffic and exchange. The physics of the system always has a psychic dimension, and the force and impact of an event must be calculated accordingly.

In addition, every normativity field has an index of volatility by degree; the degree of volatility in any system is indexed to the amount of equilibrium. Equilibrium, however, can work for or against volatility, depending on the specific constitution of what agitates the system. If the agitator is highly reactive and the equilibrium is high, the effect can be devastating. Agitants are components of the forces of affective dynamics, to which we now turn our attention.

B.4 Affective dynamics

Normativity is one form of social equilibrium, but affective dynamics and agency are less stable, more driven and can be more volatile and disruptive. The force of affect through the medium of the social can wreak havoc on an equilibrium condition. If normativity and inertia are, for better or worse, stabilizing forces, then affective dynamics are unpredictable.

Affective dynamics

Normativity, by contrast, has an inevitability to it. Normativity will occur under any set of conditions in which a relative equilibrium can occur, but affective dynamics cannot be predicted. They occur in all kinds of situations, with rapid appearance, uncertain outcomes, and across considerable distances. Normativity depends upon connections, generally within a physical environment; but affective dynamics work through communicative and media networks as well as technological, atmospheric, and infrastructural systems. For this reason affective dynamics are *the* generative force in the system of social relativity. The unpredictable outcome of elections, behavior of stock markets, and other social phenomena at scale are examples of these dynamics at work.

On a personal level, a crush, a resentment, a provocation to anger or a call to attention can work as an affective force.

The dynamic depends on the threshold of resistance and the potency of the force, as well as the circumstances of receptivity, as surely as in any other electro-magnetic-chemico-quantum physical system. But with the difference that affect functions in a non-linear manner. On a group level, affective dynamics can be generated by hysteria, mass-hallucination, small- or large-scale manipulation or response. These dynamics have almost no counter-point to stabilize them except inertia. Thus affective and inertial forces are always struggling for balance. Their constant negotiation produces the equilibrium and/or disequilibrium in any social system.

The rest of the forces are described more briefly, because their workings are component parts or qualifying features of the major forces of stabilizing inertia and affective dynamics.

B.5 Diffusion, dilution, intensification

Diffusion through social media results in shared conditions without explicit contact or apparent communication. We feel the opacity of human beings within that medium when we observe the processes by which ideas or motivations diffuse through a group. Diffusion is the simple fact of energy moving across entity boundaries through transactions; dilution diminishes the effects of such diffusion.

Dilution is the effect of energy working through a group or community and suffering the loss of some impact as a result. At a family dinner, for instance, dilution is often a useful byproduct of the increase in numbers of participants (more attendees, for instance, might distribute and therefore diminish energy felt as pressure or obligation). A particular force can only hold so long and be so strong when diluted in the diverse attentions of a group.

Diffusion

By contrast, intensification can occur when the attention of a group becomes directed or focused, growing in proportion to the number of participants, degree of directedness, duration, original force of the originating charge, and other factors. Diffusion can be incidental: walking with someone in a public space like a street or museum diffuses the one-on-one energy through a random attention field, which sitting in a booth in a restaurant concentrates that energy.

B.6 Gravity and levity

These are two major affective forces in the universe (of the first we know only a little, of the second not nearly enough). Gravity provides heft and weight, levity supplies play and movement. Gravity works as a sobering influence in inertial systems and as a braking influence on affective dynamics. Gravity and levity are rarely in equilibrium, and it could be argued that they work

Gravity and levity

Psychic bonding

with different elements of the social system, in the same ways heat and sound work with different elements of physical systems.

Still, they are constantly at work in all social systems and thus, in some significant way, they are exercising an influence on each other. Gravity has more inertia than levity. Levity requires more fuel, input, and engagement to be sustained, but can also induce slippage through a perceived insufficiency of respect. Levity can make for fluid motion, encourage momentum and change, and gravity can assert a stabilizing influence. Levity can also galvanize a situation or event in disproportion to the energy in its input—and to positive effect. But both forces are always at work. Gravity has a sinking, staying power, and is supported by and supportive of inertia, while levity runs out without ongoing energy to sustain its motion. The gravity of a memorial service slows the temporal unfolding, while the light quickness of a boat ride on a warm afternoon generates levity.

B.7 Psychic bonding and proximity dynamics

The concept of "us" is reinforced by molecular bonding, and the merging of energy fields. Proximity mixes cellular material, energy fields, pheromone realms, and other elements of the unbounded self. Some rates of exchange are volatile and very frequent, just as some materials will exchange chemical material when they are in physical contact of proximity. Frequency exchange—that is, the rate of exchange and the use of various frequencies of communication, transaction, and other channels of trade—is extremely common; it can happen even without explicit contact, through spatial proximity. Sharing a corridor, living in a neighborhood, taking the same trains—these are all opportunities for cellular mixing and aural blending. (Aura, in this sense, is not a mystical concept, but a physical one—the force field of heat, attention, communication, pheromones, touch, taste, and smell.)

In other words, the fields of dynamic engagement and exchange that are comprised by the sensorium, by cognitive processing, and by unconscious absorption and release. The force of psychic bonding is strongly felt from sharing a bed with another living entity, the illusion of boundaries dissolves in the continual energy exchange. The exchange of energy is not a transfer, but a process producing bonds, and bonds are dynamically charged, vital, and non-static. They can maintain themselves if the proximity continues, but require maintenance if a configuration changes. Bonds can be made and maintained at great distances of time and space as well. They are affected by proximity, not determined by it. Psychic bonding can also be achieved through the process of identification. But in general, proximity dynamics involve physical, literal space or intense and/or frequent exchanges in symbolic or virtual space.

Proximity dynamics are at work in configurations. Proximity can be determined as a factor of geographical, physical, temporal, eventual, circumstantial, emotional, intellectual, or mental features. Proximity does not depend upon immediacy, but instead requires a continuity of exchange, or force of attraction, or other energy in the system, if it is to be sustained. And sustained proximity is always transactional, even if rates of exchange and degrees of codependent or mutual impact vary considerably, depending on the porousness of boundaries and ratios of desire or defense.

Intimacy creates proximity bonds, but intimacy by itself will not sustain them. Intimacy can be bracketed, isolated, and compartmentalized to such a degree that it has no overflow into continuity of connection. Intimacy is an entanglement that does not require proximity, though it flourishes and strengthens or weakens and fails under proximate conditions.

B.8 Beholding

To be beheld is to be created in projection. There is a contract, implied but present, of sustenance (nurturing) and sustained engagement (bonding). Beholding also creates a being-beholden-to, that is, an obligation. This has no simple reciprocity, this co-dependence. Beholding is constitutive and relational. Being seen, being held in a gaze, being held in a psychic configuration—these are all powerful aspects of beholding.

The old patriarch, knowing all his spouses, children, grandchildren, and their histories, held them all in his gaze. When he died, the bond that held them dissolved, and though they hardly knew themselves how it happened, the framework of their connections dissolved.

B.9 Momentum

A wave function of accreted force that is fed by other factors such as desire ratios, social currency fluctuations, aspiration capacitors, and other drives that appropriate energy into the stream and keep it running, momentum can operate in any domain of the social. Momentum acts like a value added to a force, but it has a force of its own—this is clear because when it is removed, the effects and outcomes of any social dynamic shift. The momentum of a relationship can arise spontaneously, tumbling the equilibrium conditions into a state of perturbation. The stable mood of the office can turn volatile when a colleague lashes out, revealing long-pent emotion. A dating relationship can spiral down quickly at an indication of diminished interest, or, by contrast, increase in intensity from affirmation. Emotional investment

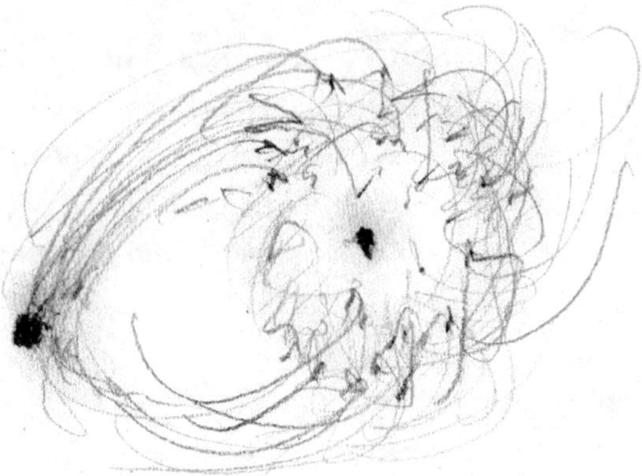

Beholding

Momentum

and mass contribute to momentum in accord with their negative and positive charge. A child coming rapidly towards you stops abruptly at a harsh tone, their momentum broken and the perturbance in the field of connection is felt immediately.

B.10 Attractors and attractions

Agential features that induce configurations, attractors have incredible power across distances. Once the distances are overcome through connection or communication, then other dynamics are able to be transacted. Transactions are enabled by attractors. Attractors are inexplicable. Someone walks into a building where you are, looks at you across a hallway, and you feel a connection, an attraction. Sometimes it plays out, sometimes not, but the feeling is distinct and can be immediate, or grow, or be discovered.

B.11 Dynamic physics of repulsion

While the identity of this force is obvious, its cause and impacts are not always linear. Repulsion is a force that turns, is easily mutated, whereas attraction has a very short half-life and often dissolves very quickly in any proximity dynamic. Repulsion can be as strong a bond as attraction, and an act of overcoming it will create a strong bond, just as resisting attraction can increase that charge. The investment in negation, the denial of repulsion, has great affective strength. Bonding to someone or a situation one does not like takes more energy than connecting through attraction, and the investment can have incredible charge as a result. We see this in the political arena, where abuse of power creates repulsion that is constantly being overcome, with powerful effects.

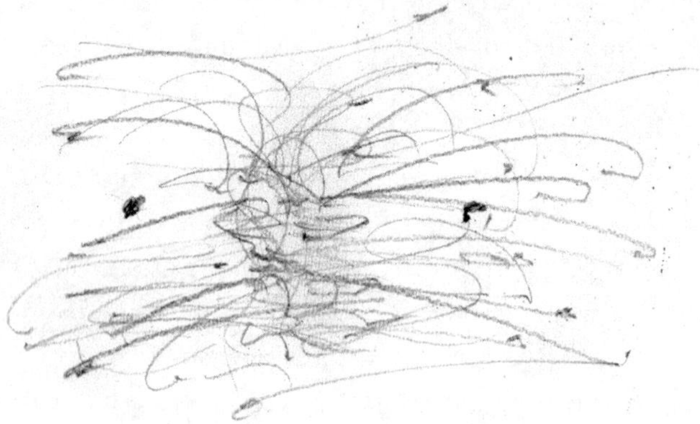

Attraction and repulsion

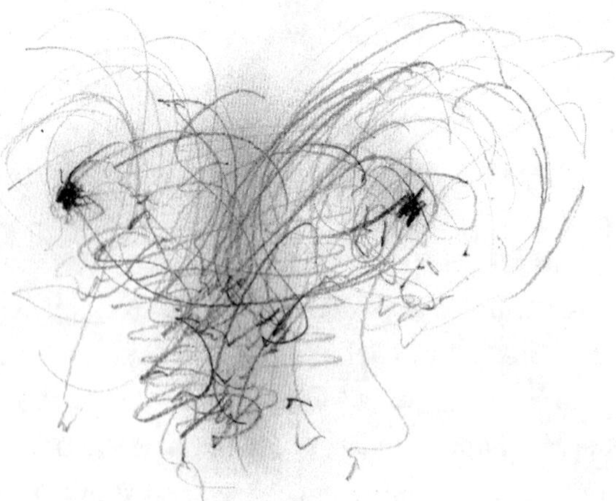

Troughs

B.12 Troughs

Troughs are negative energy spaces into which individuals, groups, and/or communities can fall. These aren't necessarily bad in terms of their impact or outcomes. They are the social equivalent of low energy systems, allowing connections to be made and configurations to occur that might not work in a more open, above-board, or apparent high-pressure circumstance. Joints and configurations created in a trough can have considerable longevity, but are more typically part of a wave function that is temporarily reconfiguring relationships (through a perturbation). A trough can develop with incredible speed: when you are sitting beside someone with whom you are entangled, and an energy space opens between you that shifts dimensions from standard metrics to affective ones. You are drawn in as surely as a hamster down an incline. A trough can be negative or positive, but it is like a rubber sheet stretching the time-space continuum. To all appearances, you and another person, sitting in a meeting, on separate institutional chairs, are simply two colleagues side by side, and yet, the personal dynamics have warped the emotional space so that you are falling into a trough of entanglement, even as you continue to sit, calmly focused on the evident agenda.

C. ATTRIBUTES OF SYSTEMS

The simplest condition of life is a transactional boundary surrounding material that sustains self-replication

Attributes are modifying or qualifying features of systems. They have some dynamic agency and force, but are dependent and descriptive (in contrast to events and forces).

C.1 Basic unboundedness

The appearance and perception of any thing as an entity—fixed, bound, and autonomous—is an illusion. The concept of unboundedness is essential to counter many simple misperceptions, such as (most obviously) the concept of bounded identity. All entities exist in a condition of codependence with their circumstances. Entities are simply the momentarily (perceptibly) static configuration of an event that is unfolding, but on a time scale that is not perceived. The fundamental tension between entities and events is a product of its codependent relation to the other full and rich complexity that is human development or processing. These two chaotic systems are stable only in the fact of their relation—but without any stability in any of the conditions of that relation. Add to this, that layer of encoded mediations that takes the form of graphical images, writing, language, notation systems of all kinds. Mediated contingencies, ephemerally stable, within tenuous but consensual notational systems; this is basic. Complexity lies in the details of each relation, each reaching equilibrium only according to a calibrated condition of particularity.

C.2 Entity illusions

Intimately related to unboundedness is the perceptual condition of the unbounded entity. Entity autonomy is fiction. The simplest condition of life is a transactional boundary surrounding material that sustains self-replication. The boundary is molecular, an alignment of chemical units facing outward and inward across which processes can be transacted. But the boundaries are always transactional, this is key, and the entity is contingent upon conditions specific to its tolerances and capacities. It lives because it has energy and can reproduce its chemical-molecular structure. Our boundedness is an illusion reinforced by mechanisms, such as photography, that produce images of discrete people. Eating, smelling, tasting—ingestion is the most obvious contradiction of boundedness, sharing warmth, touch, exchanging glances, moods, feelings, are others, and in the long sharing spaces, marriage bed, family life, sustained contact in professional or personal situations, the merging of psychic material is ongoing, and constant.

C.3 Within-ness

Epistemology from within, rather than via any subject/object distinction, is described as the domain of immanence, as within-ness. Self and knowing are co-dependent, but not identical. Knowledge produces its objects, but as a processing of the actual. Within-ness is positioned as a counterpoint to critique, a position of critical epistemology that presumes to be outside of what it addresses.[8]

C.4 Among-ness

This is a condition of sentience in which the awareness of being is awareness of being in the world, among all things, and thus situated and with an identity that does not depend upon other-ness. The specificity of identity without alterity is a condition of among-ness.

Aesthetic activity and authorial identity have generally been constructed as oppositional "othering". Literary language is often conceived as "other" than ordinary language, usually for some explicitly or implicitly "valuable" purpose, and the authorial subject (like all subjects in language) has been understood as constituted by a binary opposition to an "other" within an enunciative system.

Can these practices and identity formations be thought by means other than oppositional otherness? Is there an alternative to alterity, to the "othering" of language and the othering it enacts as enunciation? Can we posit specificity without alterity? (And might there be an eco-poetical benefit to this reformulation? By eco-poetical, I should say I mean an ecology of poeisis, making, as a system—not a poetics of ecological themes or topics. In such a formulation, identity would be construed situationally, not oppositionally. The idea of "other than" as a foundation of identity is replaced by a recognition of the specificity by which every entity is located within an ecology of identity production, with its multiplicity of positions and flows. Without binary otherness, identity become topical and positional, specific but not oppositional.) Might a political benefit be gained in the process of proposing a concept of *amongness* to replace—or at least extend—that of *otherness*?

C.5 Cognitive resonance

Cognitive resonance is the condition of communicative exchange through a system of any scale, density, complexity, or granularity that enables medial operations of the social. This is an extremely strong force and generates its own heat, energy, and momentum until it reaches an optimal condition of diffusion, and then dissipates.

D ANALYTIC AND DESCRIPTIVE METRICS

Standard metrics will not work to calculate, measure, or assess the non-mechanical phenomena of social relativity, since those processes occur at varying rates of change and are governed by affective forces. They need to be understood in non-Newtonian terms.

D.1 Affective metrics

Because all relationships are governed by principles whose particularity and specificity are determined by the infinitely scalable and always relative granularity of details, metrics that are generated by these relational conditions are affective. They do not adhere to standard metrics because they are constantly varying and modifying under various pressures. By pressure what is meant is, very simply: the stresses of human exchanges and their ever-present dis-equilibria. The force of each component is always in an uneven exchange with the others, no matter how compliant or good-natured, and thus the tensions of exchange within the system are always in dynamic play. Family systems provide very good examples of these constantly shifting conditions, and continual recalibrations of mood, attitude, and other indicators. Measuring these in any standard system would be impossible, because of the complex co-dependencies of each component and force in relation to each other. My sister and I are not in a relationship of discrete entities. In the relationship, my-sister-and-I, the two entities are constituted by the configuring relationship in all of its constant dynamics.

The effects of distortion or torque can be very minor, or they can be radical, extreme, discontinuous, asynchronous, variably uneven and so on, but—any notion of standard metrics is irrelevant within a GTSR. No relationship can be read entirely against externals, or in a system that stands outside of the relationship field itself. We can't use observer-independent, standard, metrics to calculate the constantly changing scales and changes in scale involved. Imagine the coordinates of a road map constantly redrawn according to the relative speed of every vehicle moving through it. No single Cartesian grid could be used to map those movements—because they are making the scale as they move. By analogy, affective metrics are generated as an effect of dynamic change and variability in social space. They can be abstracted, but not predicted, after their unfolding, and their eventuality can be studied from outcomes. Affective metrics are non-linear and stochastic in their character and quality, but very useful as a way of understanding loss and benefit analyses within the transactional fields that constitute the illusory boundaries of self-ness and its exchange ratios of production among other entity illusions.

D.2 Social probability

Social probability can be computed as the ratio of relative frequency and belief in possibility. Probability outcomes can be exclusive (where one or the other thing occurs), independent (where each can happen unrelatedly but together, simultaneously, asynchronously, etc.), or related (if this, then that is likely). Dispositions inflects outcomes, like whims, but more consistently and powerfully, with the potential to alter whole directional flows of energies, moods, and transactions.

D.3 Wave and particle

Because both discrete and continuous conditions are simultaneously at work in any social system, the ability to describe phenomena in these terms is essential. Waves are intuitive, and easier to grasp, as a part of diffusion or intensification: continuous conditions. Again, we are concerned with quantum processes. Waves in the medium of the social are not like waves in water, or air, but perturbances across a probabilistic distribution in a field that is comprised of forces, not simply containing them. (The same distinction applies to social space as to physical space—where space can be conceived of as an a priori existing container into which things are placed, or, as spatiality, which is always a relational effect of things positioned relative to each other. Time and temporality are distinguished in the same way.). The particle phenomena (i.e., the discrete condition) includes memes and other bits of configured thought form. Many values and beliefs circulate in particle form, even if or when they are diffused through wave patterns.

D.4 Attending to the actual

So much of what we term "the real" is merely an interface to the actual. The actual is the ever-occurring beingness in all its multiplicity and complexity. The real is a filtered version of the too-much-ness of actual phenomena, a consumable packaging created by the cognitive processors of the sensorium and their partners in perceptual crime, constructs and obstructs that model our theater of experience to pass on as real. Being able to frame analysis in terms of the actual is an essential means of escaping from deductive and inductive systems of explanation. In an abductive framework, what *is* simply *is* and all explanation is descriptive, not deterministic or capable of generating deterministic rules.

Beyond Social Mechanics

GTSR is premised on the belief that social life is not able to be explained in Newtonian terms. Critiques of rationalism abound, and have for decades or more: the well-established post-Cartesian paradigm, for instance, with its assertions that reason is a partial solution to problems that can't be formulated or addressed systematically. The rationalization of space is a perfect example.

Standard metrics organize a representation of space and project coordinates on the physical to be used for navigation and orientation, but they cannot *order* the phenomenal world.

What falls to reason to explain is what conforms to its laws. Empiricism is the refuge of the anxious, eager to secure some kind of stability against the colossal uncertainty and unpredictability of things. These are all things we know because we know how to know them. If reason is insufficient to the task before us, likewise mechanical explanations, as a subset of rational methods, also fail. The elementary criticism of science is grounded in the recognition that we only describe what we know, and that knowledge is a form of consensual ignorance capable of describing only what we can apprehend at any point in personal and historical time (once, when there were no empirically demonstrated molecules or microbes, indeed nothing smaller than what the naked eye could see, the mind imagined atoms into being, then their particles, and so on).

Newtonian methodologies analyze actions and behaviors, the dynamics of the physical world at the scale we apprehend. In this mechanical framework we are perceiving organisms programmed by the basic necessities that become sufficient. This is enough. It works. If I can survive by understanding Newton's laws of inertia, energy, reaction, mass, then why would I need to extend beyond them? Thermodynamics becomes useful later, and extends to other sufficiencies, luxuries in the survival of the organism and species. I don't need to know these laws to survive, but when I do, then advantages accrue. And quantum physics? And relativity? The multiple dimensions of the probabilistic world begin to be apparent.

As we know, the social sciences explain the manufacture of opinion and the exercise of influence in mechanical terms. Points of contact, the impact of language, the content of messages, the force of sentiment, and so on, are all analyzed through what appears to be tractable: surveys, polls, ethnographic observations, demographics, the patterns of the known and visible aspects of production and consumption, of class identity, of upbringing and values, of education, schooling, communities, religious institutions and on and on and on.

But non-Newtonian dimensions escape all notice, except in the work of dramatists, novelists, and gossip columnists, only some of whom actually have any idea of the system (rather than symptoms) they are describing. The very concept of the instrumental has be given up, recognized as inadequate. What is happening in this room, any room, any situation and circumstance? What is love, if not a spooky action?

Though still incomplete, this sketch for a GTSR is meant to provide a conceptual framework on which to begin analysis and description of the multiple dynamics and dimensions of our actual lives. As individuals and collectives we need to understand how we are subject to forces we cannot directly control, and yet of which we are a part. The construction of agency, like the engagement of understanding, only comes by negotiating the force fields of social life within a recognition of its relative dimensions. The limits of agency are far more real than we imagine, and human survival depends in part on the realization that the collective field has more power, and works through us more effectively, than we have admitted. To change its polarity, direction, orientation, or transformative motion requires alignments and aggregations to produce collective agency. The social field must make up its mind in us, through us, if we are to survive and evolve.

Cultural Melancholy

If we do not matter, it is because there is no we that still matters

Today, a pervasive individual and collective melancholy prevails. The sense of loss proceeds from a conviction that the scale of devastation is much larger than we realize. A friend stops me in the street, walking his dog. He says, referencing a cultural moment decades earlier as if it provides a model for our actions now, "We stopped a war." But the political administration of the nineteen-seventies, for all of its abuses, still functioned on terms of accountability—not, necessarily to a social contract, but to a sense that language had an actual relation to a referent and that actions had a directed relation to outcomes.

That is long gone, gone certainly by the first Gulf War in the nineteen-nineties. The events of 9/11 and following undid what remained. We moved into the fully phantasmatic, what used to be termed the "simulacral", when other structures of reference were still in place.

Now we function through our shared addiction to a symbolism that is all surface symptoms. The weapons of mass destruction, shock and awe, all that sick hyperbole of the period at the turn of the millennium didn't just warp, but in fact marked the distance between public discourse and actuality. We knew that.[9] But the disruptions in the political field, the full extent of perturbations created for the sake of destabilization, destructive chaos, wanton unpredictability and shape-shifting purpose, were less apparent.

Now?

The already-over past-ness of our present feels palpable, thick with portents and inevitability, the momentum of unraveling. The institutions of education, justice, equity, social fairness, safety, well being, care, humanity—all eroded, and alongside them the tragedy of the earth unfolds. No wonder we are weary, melancholic, and even if not bitter or despairing, are weighed down with the realization that all that we value and have valued is at risk. High risk. Likely extinction.

So what we register is loss. The too-lateness of regret, the impotence of reconsideration, and the brutal reality of everything we have enjoyed as privilege being eclipsed by destructive forces. Our precariousness and our expendability are intertwined even as protests against the forces of destruction spring up spontaneously, trying to keep civility alive. If we do not matter, it is because there is no *we* that still matters. Humanity has become a surplus that adds no value to the various systems of which it used to seem to be a crucial part.

My mid-century generation was born into a wave of unexamined collective optimism, fed on the engines of effluvia that swelled possibilities beyond precedent. We saw the earth as a platform, a launch point, saw the transformations of materials into products as the drive of petroleum towards self-realization in synthetics designed to shape a world that fit them. Possibilities multiplied, dimensions opened. We who came of age without knowing The War, as we used to call WWII, or the Depression, without the direct experience of suffering and deprivation, imagined it might always be so, on this continent, with our buffering strength and will to global expansion justified as a right and exercised by virtue of the outcome of our perceived triumphs. Economic power sanctified political conditions. Colonialism squared and made itself into corporate systems, networks of trade, extended elaborate means of exploitation masquerading as imports and exports, all contributed to the favorable balance sheet tipped in our direction. We profited, complicit without acknowledgment, in the boom cycles that mapped themselves as if natural onto the suburbs and exurbs of literal and virtual space. Interiority turned outward, the exhalation of breath a relief from holding back against the swelling tide of recreational consumption now rampant.

The bloated world expanded, we separated from ourselves, spots on an inflated surface, pulling our minds from our bodies, our spirits from our tasks, our sense of purpose from the aspirations to succeed and then celebritize. Full bellies, starving psyches, ever eager for more, we attach ourselves to fame and commoditize, leveraging whatever future might be bartered or bet in exchange. Assassinations and deaths, early graves and tragic figures, signaled not their demise but ours, in the sense that we saw the end of innocence, the final throes of our capacity to believe in any actual civic spirit or social contract. Social infrastructure erodes, corrodes, dissolves, and (as they say), the center will not hold. We witness the gradual and then increasingly accelerated downfall of once sincere aspirations. If this is not what the beginning of the end looks like, then what does?

Melancholics live between anticipation and regret. That between-ness is a gap now closing. Anticipation vanishes, its illusions unsustainable. The late stage of decadence bedevils us. How to sort through the confusions of past fixes to surface symptoms of a deep malaise. More could be said (and will be said), but nothing changes the recognition that what we register is loss. The too-lateness of everything, not individually, but collectively, staring into the new void with an equally new level of disbelief.

A single report brings the present into snapshot focus, the sharp slap of gestalt: Refugees on land, their sea ice gone, the bears wander in confusion. Our confusion. Now visited on them. Violent adaptation takes more than a generation. We processed permission and thought it was structural change, mistaking opportunities for rights. (My female body was mine, so rare in the history of humankind. Backlash revenge, the will of which people?)

The criminalization of knowledge is one aspect of our cultural crisis, perhaps the tip of an iceberg vanishing under the heat of aggressive ignorance. Denial is a stalling tactic out of synch with the pace of what it denies, since the scale of destruction makes it invisible from where we sit. Our position is inadequate to the task of grasping the full complexity: multiple, full worlds along manifold axes of unfolding in fields that proliferate variation in speeds, rates, conditions of their own realization, unleashed, unfathomable, and very certainly long out of control. What relativities are at work, and what intuitions give us access to their workings? Start with some statements about how to understand phenomena within their specificity, or, attend to the specificity of the act of apprehension in its production of the phenomenal actualities in their apparent and relative dimensions.

These are not yet the darkest times. These are moments when the light is diminishing.

After Speaking in Tongues

Take sound from air and human speech, in acts of subtractive poetics, and the leftover space is scant. We suck the pauses up, search for intervals, in need of non-existent desperate silence. The earth wobbles on its turn, still a little more inhabitable than the dry dust planets cracking with ice, little sub-worlds, far away, relatively speaking—and speaking they are. The standing up of machines on their hind legs frees their jointed arms for food gathering and more speaking, gesturing, making signs out of that same air that breaks with sound waves and patterns in mind and mined fields. No agriculture troubles their brows, only the furrowing lines of engines plowing the lawns and churning the earth into lines of text, unreadable but semiotic none-the-less. The soil turning makes only a soft blanket hush that never disturbs the gears of the equipment. The song they were singing was made of compressed air, so light the melody hung on the breeze and rippled across the lanes of traffic the barking dogs the engine noises and the roar of city services.

Our backyard orchestra has gone to sleep already, dawn chorus subsides and an opera drawn from life is not quite the experience of a lifetime. Cats will and possums do and squirrels as well, but the noise from leaf blowers tops them all. The machines are winning, and many of them are no longer made of moving parts. They sigh and wiggle and work their way into our affections without any need for lubrication.

Poetics grows up domesticated like a dog, its bark reverberating in a group, then on a stage, holding forth. With meter and metrics the art advances, structured from body breath and motion, the short bursts and the long holding, the exhalation and the inward draw, into the chest, into the stomach, feet, hands. The stomping effect of form on language makes it perform like song.

All that went on a long time, after all, and the somatic pleasures of verse account in some large part for its popularity, letting the tricks of staccato and accent roll around in the mouth and on the tongue. The meaning of verse is an effect, but its metric is the fact of its sound. On it goes, into shape-forms, numbers of this and that, circumscribed, proscribed, adhered to. Dance steps for the intellect. Perform accordingly. Alterations and exchanges.

Forms also come in the luggage, hitch a ride on a trade route, get noticed at court, picked up off the street, overheard in the market, found in the back rooms, the bar rooms, the public square. The whole panoply of possibilities is populated by variant species of some things that are the same and some that are other. Human speech, humans speaking, that prevails, even with the use of drums, guitars, the flutes and clarinets that take our breath away, even with all of these, overarching them all is speech. Acts. Language. Synthesizer.

The final transition to a light load on a heavy processor outputs as simulation. We don't mind, amused by the voice that is not ever ours. The machines should be allowed to talk, to us, for us, with us, their servile guiding tone, responsive to requests. Not a threat. Not even a hint or whisper of an intelligence comes through. Nor should it. The sub-sub-level of production is in the offering to use, in the new vocabulary of out-sourced sound files and types, tones of inaudible and audible outputs that take their place alongside the sighing springs and snapped elastics of an earlier era.

Not the language of machines, not language in machines, not language coming into or out of machines, but the very takeover of sound-noise rhythms of the material world—animate, inanimate, mechanic, organic–produced how where, and so our self-adjusting ears adapt and produce alternate interiorities and external vibrations unlike the other sounds of prior utterance. A helicopter overhead beats with its wings and praises its own song. The noise music and the sound forms all escape and make new waves into the world. Our transformation hardly matters and goes with little notice unspoken, unsung.

The time of tongues is past.

Appendix: Formulations of the General Theory

This sample set of formulae were created simply to demonstrate that the General Theory of Social Relativity can be put into mathematical and computable forms, as a set of principles whose dynamics work simultaneously at a level of specificity and of abstraction. Any and every concrete instance of social relations can be described within the theory of social relativity, and a formulaic analysis of the dynamics at work can be generated that takes into account the general principles and the anomalies of the specific instantiation in an event.

The Basic Formulation

$$R \longrightarrow \varepsilon = (\int) [\delta (\Omega{:}\rho+\rho...) / \phi (A{:}\rho+\rho...)] + f\rho$$

The equation can be interpreted as the expression of proximity/frequency ratios for optimal equilibrium in which any relationship can stabilize based on how often and how close the connections are:

> Any relationship, R, approaches equilibrium(ε) as a function($\int$) of the relation between distance (delta / δ) and frequency (phi / φ), where each can be modified by a constant (Omega/ Ω for distance or Alpha /A for frequency) de-

I knew there had to be an explanation for why I go on so well with my brother-in-law after he moved to Texas and I stayed in Duluth and only saw him twice after that, at my niece's wedding six years later, and then at his funeral.

termined in relation to particulars (rho / $\rho+\rho$...) specific to the case. Friction, (fr), a non-productive by-product, is sometimes released and sometimes simply generated in the process. In some cases, distance has to approach infinity and frequency approach zero for equilibrium to occur. Many other modifications of this basic theory, whose iterative versions describe relational stability and equilibrium in all social phenomena, will be shown in other formulae. Every relationship can reach equilibrium given the right ratio of proximity and frequency (approaching distant/intimate and never/constant as limits), though the toxic by-products might be considerable.

Social Systems Processes

$S/sys\ P \ \tilde{}{=}\ \tilde{}\ E\ (\Sigma : \lambda(cg\gamma))$

Social systems processes (S/sys P) are (vaguely) equivalent (vaguely because equivalence is by definition not calculable or possible in the GTSR) where the energy (E) is always modulating in a transaction exchange (Sigma) calculated as a set of qualifications (lambda) modified by coefficients (Chi) to the power of their details (gamma gamma). This describes the way energy works in transactions.

Normalcy

$N = (A^{n + iii...} / (\Delta / \gamma)\ C{\sim})\ t$

Normalcy (N) equals any set of assumptions (A) or operative values raised to the power of the number of individuals in any group ($^{ii+iii...}$), divided by a factor of (population density divided by the amount of geography occupied) (Δ/γ) with a constant (X) that allows for deviation from the norm calculated as a demographic variable. All of this has to be calculated in relation to the time of the system's duration vs. amount of internal change to the conditions (τ). Normalcy will be perturbed if radical shifts in demographics occur, but will remain remarkably stable, and repressive, if the system's composition remains the same. Repressive forces generated by normalcy are perceptible.

Notes

1. Speculative realism arose as an alternative to the longstanding distinction between thinking and being that is linked to Immanuel Kant and the idea of a correlation between thought and the real (or, at least, the perceived). The question of how we can know drives speculative realism towards non-correlative approaches. I see some strong affinities between that attitude and the "non-representational" approach at the core of my work in modeling visualizations. But the issues I am trying to address in the General Theory are not those of how we know, but more pragmatically, they are issues of how what we know needs rethinking and a shift from classical to quantum approaches for analysis of social processes. Similarly, in spite of the richness of new materialist approaches to the agency of matter, material systems, and other non-human components of the world, their explanations provide only a partial insight into the workings of the social medium as I am outlining its properties and operations. When my colleague, Jerome McGann, and I began the Speculative Computing Lab at the University of Virginia in 2000, Speculative realism was still several years in the future (the Goldsmiths' conference was in 2007, though I had no idea about its principles until about 2009-10). Our engagement with speculative thought arose directly from reading quantum theory, which we were applying to the problems of interpretation, textual criticism, and the way to model theoretical practice within

a digital environment. Those formulations thread through *SpecLab* (2009) and *What Is?* (2013) The distance between those texts and the concepts of Speculative realism is clear—and remains. The book *Stochastic Poetics* (2010-2012) and the project *Subjective Meteorology* both show aspects of the General Theory, but both are difficult to find (they are in small, limited, rare editions) and their theoretical formulations are hard to decipher within their poetic expressions. All of this is by way of acknowledging the evident parallels between the General Theory and other current investigations of knowledge, processes, systems theory, and my own work. Though I have not read it, the work of Alexander Wendt, of which I have only just become aware (*Quantum Mind*, 2015), seems to have the strongest affinity with what I am attempting.

2. The social has always operated as the phantasmatic, but mass mediation, telecommunications, and the transactional intensification they produce have escalated the forces at work in the field.
3. See Drucker, "Stochastic Poetics and Diagrammatic Writing," *The Iowa Review*, Volume 44, Issue 3, Winter 2014/15.
4. Two Atlantic articles provided information on Surtov:

   https://www.theatlantic.com/international/archive/2014/11/hidden-author-putinism-russia-vladislav-surkov/382489/
   https://www.theatlantic.com/international/archive/2014/09/russia-putin-revolutionizing-information-warfare/379880/
5. See Appendix for formulation.
6. See Appendix for formulation.
7. Asking these questions in a conversation with a sociologist/media theorist in California, I was confronted with resistance. He said every aspect of the phenomena I was describing could be explained with empirical study and analysis of transactions and interactions. He felt that the socializing effects of each

exchange would, if properly logged and described, account for the normalization. He was convinced that a mechanical explanation could suffice, if it were sufficiently detailed. He refused to entertain the idea of a phenomenon that was an aggregate that had an existence beyond individual experience, but as a result of it. The concept of a social atmosphere created by the combination of exchanges, that became its own field of charges, he condemned as magical thinking.

8. Like many points here, this could support a longer elaboration.
9. I wrote *Deterring Discourse* as an expression of that disconnect and frustration.